# Connected Mathematics 2

# What Do You Expect?

## Probability and Expected Value

Glenda Lappan

James T. Fey

William M. Fitzgerald

Susan N. Friel

Elizabeth Difanis Phillips

PEARSON

Boston, Massachusetts · Glenview, Illinois · Shoreview, Minnesota · Upper Saddle River, New Jersey

Connected Mathematics™ was developed at Michigan State University with financial support from the Michigan State University Office of the Provost, Computing and Technology, and the College of Natural Science.

This material is based upon work supported by the National Science Foundation under Grant No. MDR 9150217 and Grant No. ESI 9986372. Opinions expressed are those of the authors and not necessarily those of the Foundation.

The Michigan State University authors and administration have agreed that all MSU royalties arising from this publication will be devoted to purposes supported by the MSU Mathematics Education Enrichment Fund.

**Acknowledgments** appear on page 74, which constitutes an extension of this copyright page.

13-digit ISBN  978-0-13-366144-6
10-digit ISBN  0-13-366144-X

9  10  V003  15 14

# Authors of Connected Mathematics

*(from left to right)* Glenda Lappan, Betty Phillips, Susan Friel, Bill Fitzgerald, Jim Fey

**Glenda Lappan** is a University Distinguished Professor in the Department of Mathematics at Michigan State University. Her research and development interests are in the connected areas of students' learning of mathematics and mathematics teachers' professional growth and change related to the development and enactment of K–12 curriculum materials.

**James T. Fey** is a Professor of Curriculum and Instruction and Mathematics at the University of Maryland. His consistent professional interest has been development and research focused on curriculum materials that engage middle and high school students in problem-based collaborative investigations of mathematical ideas and their applications.

**William M. Fitzgerald** *(Deceased)* was a Professor in the Department of Mathematics at Michigan State University. His early research was on the use of concrete materials in supporting student learning and led to the development of teaching materials for laboratory environments. Later he helped develop a teaching model to support student experimentation with mathematics.

**Susan N. Friel** is a Professor of Mathematics Education in the School of Education at the University of North Carolina at Chapel Hill. Her research interests focus on statistics education for middle-grade students and, more broadly, on teachers' professional development and growth in teaching mathematics K–8.

**Elizabeth Difanis Phillips** is a Senior Academic Specialist in the Mathematics Department of Michigan State University. She is interested in teaching and learning mathematics for both teachers and students. These interests have led to curriculum and professional development projects at the middle school and high school levels, as well as projects related to the teaching and learning of algebra across the grades.

# CMP2 Development Staff

# Field Test Sites for CMP2

During the development of the revised edition of *Connected Mathematics* (CMP2), more than 100 classroom teachers have field-tested materials at 49 school sites in 12 states and the District of Columbia. This classroom testing occurred over three academic years (2001 through 2004), allowing careful study of the effectiveness of each of the 24 units that comprise the program. A special thanks to the students and teachers at these pilot schools.

## Arkansas
**Magnolia Public Schools**
Kittena Bell*, Judith Trowell*; *Central Elementary School:* Maxine Broom, Betty Eddy, Tiffany Fallin, Bonnie Flurry, Carolyn Monk, Elizabeth Tye; *Magnolia Junior High School:* Monique Bryan, Ginger Cook, David Graham, Shelby Lamkin

## Colorado
**Boulder Public Schools**
*Nevin Platt Middle School:* Judith Koenig

**St. Vrain Valley School District, Longmont**
*Westview Middle School:* Colleen Beyer, Kitty Canupp, Ellie Decker*, Peggy McCarthy, Tanya deNobrega, Cindy Payne, Ericka Pilon, Andrew Roberts

## District of Columbia
*Capitol Hill Day School:* Ann Lawrence

## Georgia
**University of Georgia, Athens**
Brad Findell

**Madison Public Schools**
*Morgan County Middle School:* Renee Burgdorf, Lynn Harris, Nancy Kurtz, Carolyn Stewart

## Maine
**Falmouth Public Schools**
*Falmouth Middle School:* Donna Erikson, Joyce Hebert, Paula Hodgkins, Rick Hogan, David Legere, Cynthia Martin, Barbara Stiles, Shawn Towle*

## Michigan
**Portland Public Schools**
*Portland Middle School:* Mark Braun, Holly DeRosia, Kathy Dole*, Angie Foote, Teri Keusch, Tammi Wardwell

**Traverse City Area Public Schools**
*Bertha Vos Elementary:* Kristin Sak; *Central Grade School:* Michelle Clark; Jody Meyers; *Eastern Elementary:* Karrie Tufts; *Interlochen Elementary:* Mary McGee-Cullen; *Long Lake Elementary:* Julie Faulkner*, Charlie Maxbauer, Katherine Sleder; *Norris Elementary:* Hope Slanaker; *Oak Park Elementary:* Jessica Steed; *Traverse Heights Elementary:* Jennifer Wolfert; *Westwoods Elementary:* Nancy Conn; *Old Mission Peninsula School:* Deb Larimer; *Traverse City East Junior High:* Ivanka Berkshire, Ruthanne Kladder, Jan Palkowski, Jane Peterson, Mary Beth Schmitt; *Traverse City West Junior High:* Dan Fouch*, Ray Fouch

**Sturgis Public Schools**
*Sturgis Middle School:* Ellen Eisele

## Minnesota
**Burnsville School District 191**
*Hidden Valley Elementary:* Stephanie Cin, Jane McDevitt

**Hopkins School District 270**
*Alice Smith Elementary:* Sandra Cowing, Kathleen Gustafson, Martha Mason, Scott Stillman; *Eisenhower Elementary:* Chad Bellig, Patrick Berger, Nancy Glades, Kye Johnson, Shane Wasserman, Victoria Wilson; *Gatewood Elementary:* Sarah Ham, Julie Kloos, Janine Pung, Larry Wade; *Glen Lake Elementary:* Jacqueline Cramer, Kathy Hering, Cecelia Morris, Robb Trenda; *Katherine Curren Elementary:* Diane Bancroft, Sue DeWit, John Wilson; *L. H. Tanglen Elementary:* Kevin Athmann, Lisa Becker, Mary LaBelle, Kathy Rezac, Roberta Severson; *Meadowbrook Elementary:* Jan Gauger, Hildy Shank, Jessica Zimmerman; *North Junior High:* Laurel Hahn, Kristin Lee, Jodi Markuson, Bruce Mestemacher, Laurel Miller, Bonnie Rinker, Jeannine Salzer, Sarah Shafer, Cam Stottler; *West Junior High:* Alicia Beebe, Kristie Earl, Nobu Fujii, Pam Georgetti, Susan Gilbert, Regina Nelson Johnson, Debra Lindstrom, Michele Luke*, Jon Sorenson

**Minneapolis School District 1**
*Ann Sullivan K-8 School:* Bronwyn Collins; Anne Bartel* (Curriculum and Instruction Office)

**Wayzata School District 284**
*Central Middle School:* Sarajane Myers, Dan Nielsen, Tanya Ravenholdt

**White Bear Lake School District 624**
*Central Middle School:* Amy Jorgenson, Michelle Reich, Brenda Sammon

## New York
**New York City Public Schools**
*IS 89:* Yelena Aynbinder, Chi-Man Ng, Nina Rapaport, Joel Spengler, Phyllis Tam*, Brent Wyso; *Wagner Middle School:* Jason Appel, Intissar Fernandez, Yee Gee Get, Richard Goldstein, Irving Marcus, Sue Norton, Bernadita Owens, Jennifer Rehn*, Kevin Yuhas

---

* indicates a Field Test Site Coordinator

### Ohio

**Talawanda School District, Oxford**
*Talawanda Middle School:* Teresa Abrams, Larry Brock, Heather Brosey, Julie Churchman, Monna Even, Karen Fitch, Bob George, Amanda Klee, Pat Meade, Sandy Montgomery, Barbara Sherman, Lauren Steidl

**Miami University**
Jeffrey Wanko*

**Springfield Public Schools**
*Rockway School:* Jim Mamer

### Pennsylvania

**Pittsburgh Public Schools**
Kenneth Labuskes, Marianne O'Connor, Mary Lynn Raith*; *Arthur J. Rooney Middle School:* David Hairston, Stamatina Mousetis, Alfredo Zangaro; *Frick International Studies Academy:* Suzanne Berry, Janet Falkowski, Constance Finseth, Romika Hodge, Frank Machi; *Reizenstein Middle School:* Jeff Baldwin, James Brautigam, Lorena Burnett, Glen Cobbett, Michael Jordan, Margaret Lazur, Melissa Munnell, Holly Neely, Ingrid Reed, Dennis Reft

### Texas

**Austin Independent School District**
*Bedichek Middle School:* Lisa Brown, Jennifer Glasscock, Vicki Massey

**El Paso Independent School District**
*Cordova Middle School:* Armando Aguirre, Anneliesa Durkes, Sylvia Guzman, Pat Holguin*, William Holguin, Nancy Nava, Laura Orozco, Michelle Peña, Roberta Rosen, Patsy Smith, Jeremy Wolf

**Plano Independent School District**
Patt Henry, James Wohlgehagen*; *Frankford Middle School:* Mandy Baker, Cheryl Butsch, Amy Dudley, Betsy Eshelman, Janet Greene, Cort Haynes, Kathy Letchworth, Kay Marshall, Kelly McCants, Amy Reck, Judy Scott, Syndy Snyder, Lisa Wang; *Wilson Middle School:* Darcie Bane, Amanda Bedenko, Whitney Evans, Tonelli Hatley, Sarah (Becky) Higgs, Kelly Johnston, Rebecca McElligott, Kay Neuse, Cheri Slocum, Kelli Straight

### Washington

**Evergreen School District**
*Shahala Middle School:* Nicole Abrahamsen, Terry Coon*, Carey Doyle, Sheryl Drechsler, George Gemma, Gina Helland, Amy Hilario, Darla Lidyard, Sean McCarthy, Tilly Meyer, Willow Neuwelt, Todd Parsons, Brian Pederson, Stan Posey, Shawn Scott, Craig Sjoberg, Lynette Sundstrom, Charles Switzer, Luke Youngblood

### Wisconsin

**Beaver Dam Unified School District**
*Beaver Dam Middle School:* Jim Braemer, Jeanne Frick, Jessica Greatens, Barbara Link, Dennis McCormick, Karen Michels, Nancy Nichols*, Nancy Palm, Shelly Stelsel, Susan Wiggins

---

* indicates a Field Test Site Coordinator

## Reviews of CMP to Guide Development of CMP2

**B**efore writing for CMP2 began or field tests were conducted, the first edition of *Connected Mathematics* was submitted to the mathematics faculties of school districts from many parts of the country and to 80 individual reviewers for extensive comments.

## School District Survey Reviews of CMP

### Arizona
Madison School District #38 (Phoenix)

### Arkansas
Cabot School District, Little Rock School District, Magnolia School District

### California
Los Angeles Unified School District

### Colorado
St. Vrain Valley School District (Longmont)

### Florida
Leon County Schools (Tallahassee)

### Illinois
School District #21 (Wheeling)

### Indiana
Joseph L. Block Junior High (East Chicago)

### Kentucky
Fayette County Public Schools (Lexington)

### Maine
Selection of Schools

### Massachusetts
Selection of Schools

### Michigan
Sparta Area Schools

### Minnesota
Hopkins School District

### Texas
Austin Independent School District, The El Paso Collaborative for Academic Excellence, Plano Independent School District

### Wisconsin
Platteville Middle School

# Individual Reviewers of CMP

**Arkansas**
Deborah Cramer; Robby Frizzell *(Taylor)*; Lowell Lynde *(University of Arkansas, Monticello)*; Leigh Manzer *(Norfork)*; Lynne Roberts *(Emerson High School, Emerson)*; Tony Timms *(Cabot Public Schools)*; Judith Trowell *(Arkansas Department of Higher Education)*

**California**
José Alcantar *(Gilroy)*; Eugenie Belcher *(Gilroy)*; Marian Pasternack *(Lowman M. S. T. Center, North Hollywood)*; Susana Pezoa *(San Jose)*; Todd Rabusin *(Hollister)*; Margaret Siegfried *(Ocala Middle School, San Jose)*; Polly Underwood *(Ocala Middle School, San Jose)*

**Colorado**
Janeane Golliher *(St. Vrain Valley School District, Longmont)*; Judith Koenig *(Nevin Platt Middle School, Boulder)*

**Florida**
Paige Loggins *(Swift Creek Middle School, Tallahassee)*

**Illinois**
Jan Robinson *(School District #21, Wheeling)*

**Indiana**
Frances Jackson *(Joseph L. Block Junior High, East Chicago)*

**Kentucky**
Natalee Feese *(Fayette County Public Schools, Lexington)*

**Maine**
Betsy Berry *(Maine Math & Science Alliance, Augusta)*

**Maryland**
Joseph Gagnon *(University of Maryland, College Park)*; Paula Maccini *(University of Maryland, College Park)*

**Massachusetts**
George Cobb *(Mt. Holyoke College, South Hadley)*; Cliff Kanold *(University of Massachusetts, Amherst)*

**Michigan**
Mary Bouck *(Farwell Area Schools)*; Carol Dorer *(Slauson Middle School, Ann Arbor)*; Carrie Heaney *(Forsythe Middle School, Ann Arbor)*; Ellen Hopkins *(Clague Middle School, Ann Arbor)*; Teri Keusch *(Portland Middle School, Portland)*; Valerie Mills *(Oakland Schools, Waterford)*; Mary Beth Schmitt *(Traverse City East Junior High, Traverse City)*; Jack Smith *(Michigan State University, East Lansing)*; Rebecca Spencer *(Sparta Middle School, Sparta)*; Ann Marie Nicoll Turner *(Tappan Middle School, Ann Arbor)*; Scott Turner *(Scarlett Middle School, Ann Arbor)*

**Minnesota**
Margarita Alvarez *(Olson Middle School, Minneapolis)*; Jane Amundson *(Nicollet Junior High, Burnsville)*; Anne Bartel *(Minneapolis Public Schools)*; Gwen Ranzau Campbell *(Sunrise Park Middle School, White Bear Lake)*; Stephanie Cin *(Hidden Valley Elementary, Burnsville)*; Joan Garfield *(University of Minnesota, Minneapolis)*; Gretchen Hall *(Richfield Middle School, Richfield)*; Jennifer Larson *(Olson Middle School, Minneapolis)*; Michele Luke *(West Junior High, Minnetonka)*; Jeni Meyer *(Richfield Junior High, Richfield)*; Judy Pfingsten *(Inver Grove Heights Middle School, Inver Grove Heights)*; Sarah Shafer *(North Junior High, Minnetonka)*; Genni Steele *(Central Middle School, White Bear Lake)*; Victoria Wilson *(Eisenhower Elementary, Hopkins)*; Paul Zorn *(St. Olaf College, Northfield)*

**New York**
Debra Altenau-Bartolino *(Greenwich Village Middle School, New York)*; Doug Clements *(University of Buffalo)*; Francis Curcio *(New York University, New York)*; Christine Dorosh *(Clinton School for Writers, Brooklyn)*; Jennifer Rehn *(East Side Middle School, New York)*; Phyllis Tam *(IS 89 Lab School, New York)*;

Marie Turini *(Louis Armstrong Middle School, New York)*; Lucy West *(Community School District 2, New York)*; Monica Witt *(Simon Baruch Intermediate School 104, New York)*

**Pennsylvania**
Robert Aglietti *(Pittsburgh)*; Sharon Mihalich *(Pittsburgh)*; Jennifer Plumb *(South Hills Middle School, Pittsburgh)*; Mary Lynn Raith *(Pittsburgh Public Schools)*

**Texas**
Michelle Bittick *(Austin Independent School District)*; Margaret Cregg *(Plano Independent School District)*; Sheila Cunningham *(Klein Independent School District)*; Judy Hill *(Austin Independent School District)*; Patricia Holguin *(El Paso Independent School District)*; Bonnie McNemar *(Arlington)*; Kay Neuse *(Plano Independent School District)*; Joyce Polanco *(Austin Independent School District)*; Marge Ramirez *(University of Texas at El Paso)*; Pat Rossman *(Baker Campus, Austin)*; Cindy Schimek *(Houston)*; Cynthia Schneider *(Charles A. Dana Center, University of Texas at Austin)*; Uri Treisman *(Charles A. Dana Center, University of Texas at Austin)*; Jacqueline Weilmuenster *(Grapevine-Colleyville Independent School District)*; LuAnn Weynand *(San Antonio)*; Carmen Whitman *(Austin Independent School District)*; James Wohlgehagen *(Plano Independent School District)*

**Washington**
Ramesh Gangolli *(University of Washington, Seattle)*

**Wisconsin**
Susan Lamon *(Marquette University, Hales Corner)*; Steve Reinhart *(retired, Chippewa Falls Middle School, Eau Claire)*

# Table of Contents

# What Do You Expect?
## Probability and Expected Value

# What Do You Expect?

## Probability and Expected Value

**I**n Raymundo's *Prime Number Multiplication Game*, a player rolls two number cubes. Player A gets 10 points if the product is prime. Player B gets 1 point if the product is not prime. Is Raymundo's game a fair game?

**I**n the district finals, Nishi has just been fouled. She gets to try one free throw. If she makes it, she gets to try a second free throw. Nishi's free-throw average is 60%. Is Nishi most likely to score 0, 1, or 2 points?

**H**ave you ever had to guess at the answers on a quiz? If you take a four-question true/false quiz and guess on every question, what are your chances of getting every question right?

Probabilities can help you make decisions. If there is a 75% chance of rain, you might decide to carry an umbrella. If a baseball player has a .245 batting average, you expect that he is more likely not to get a hit than to get a hit on a given at-bat.

Probabilities can also help you to predict what will happen over the long run. Suppose you and a friend toss a coin before each bus ride to decide who will sit by the window. You can predict that, over the long run, you will sit by the window about half of the time.

Many probability situations involve a payoff—points scored in a game, lives saved by promoting good health, or profit earned from a business venture. You can sometimes find the long-term average payoff called the expected value. For example, when deciding whether to make an investment, a company might figure out how much it can expect to earn over the long run.

In this unit, you will look at questions involving probability and expected value, including the three questions on the opposite page.

# Mathematical Highlights

## Probability and Expected Value

**I**n *What Do You Expect?*, you will deepen your understanding of basic probability concepts. You will learn about the expected value of situations involving chance.

---

**You will learn how to**

- Interpret experimental and theoretical probabilities and the relationship between them
- Distinguish between equally likely and non-equally likely events
- Review strategies for identifying possible outcomes and analyzing probabilities, such as using lists or tree diagrams
- Determine if a game is fair or unfair
- Analyze situations that involve two stages (or actions)
- Use area models to analyze situations that involve two stages
- Determine the expected value of a probability situation
- Analyze situations that involve binomial outcomes
- Use probability and expected value to make decisions

**As you work on problems in this unit, ask yourself questions about situations that involve analyzing probabilities:**

*What are the possible outcomes for the event(s) in this situation?*

*Are these outcomes equally likely?*

*Is this a fair or unfair situation?*

*Can I compute the theoretical probabilities or do I conduct an experiment?*

*How can I determine the probability of the outcome of one event followed by a second event?*

*How can I use expected value to help me make decisions?*

# Evaluating Games of Chance

**M**any board games or computer games that you play involve chance. In some games, the square you land on depends on what numbers come up when you roll a pair of number cubes. Suppose you want to roll a sum of 10.

*What is the probability that you will roll a sum of 10 on your turn?*

In *How Likely Is It?*, you played the Roller Derby game, which involves finding the sum of two number cubes. You played the game several times and computed the **experimental probability** for each sum. To find the experimental probability of getting a sum of 10, you can use this formula:

$$P(\text{sum of 10}) = \frac{\text{number of times the sum of 10 occurred}}{\text{total number of trials}}$$

You also computed **theoretical probabilities** by listing all the possible outcomes. There are 36 outcomes, three of which result in a sum of 10.

*What are the three ways in which you can get a sum of 10 when you roll a pair of number cubes?*

The theoretical probability of getting a sum of 10 is

$$P(\text{sum of 10}) = \frac{\text{number of possible outcomes with a sum of 10}}{\text{total number of possible outcomes}} = \frac{3}{36} \text{ or } \frac{1}{12}$$

In this Investigation, you will explore several games involving chance. In each situation, you are asked to determine the chance, or probability, that certain outcomes will occur. In some situations, you will also be asked to determine whether a particular game is fair.

*What do you think it means for a game to be fair?*

## 1.1 Matching Colors

April and Tioko invented a two-player spinner game called Match/No-Match.

- Players take turns spinning a spinner like the one shown here.

- On each turn, a player spins the pointer of the spinner twice. If both spins land on the same color (a match), then Player A scores 1 point. If the two spins land on different colors (a no-match), then Player B scores 2 points.

- The player with the most points after 24 spins wins.

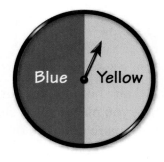

*Do you think this is a fair or unfair game?*

*Are both players equally likely to win?*

### Problem 1.1 Experimental and Theoretical Probability

- Play the Match/No-Match game with a partner. Take a total of 24 turns (12 for each player).

- For each turn, record the color pair, for example, blue-yellow. Award points to the appropriate player.

**For:** Designer Dart Boards
**Visit:** PHSchool.com
**Web Code:** and-7101

**A.** Use the results you collect to find the experimental probabilities for a match and a no-match.

**B. 1.** List all of the possible outcomes of a turn (2 spins).

   **2.** Use the possible outcomes to determine the theoretical probability of a match and a no-match.

   **3.** Are the outcomes *equally likely*? That is, does each outcome have the same chance of occurring?

**C.** Compare the experimental and theoretical probabilities.

**D.** Is Match/No-Match a fair game? If it is fair, explain why. If it is not fair, explain how the rules can be changed to make the game fair.

**ACE** Homework starts on page 10.

**I**n *How Likely Is It?*, you learned to find all the possible outcomes of a situation by making an organized list. April uses a tree diagram to show all the possible outcomes for the Match/No-Match game.

First, she lists the equally likely outcomes of the first spin.

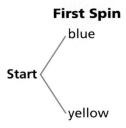

From each result of the first spin, April draws and labels two branches to show the possible results of the second spin.

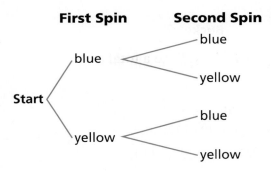

April can read all the possible outcomes of a turn by following the paths from left to right. For example, she can follow the upper branch from start to blue, and then from there, she can follow the upper branch to blue. This path represents the outcome blue-blue. The right column below lists the possible outcomes. The outcomes are all equally likely.

| First Spin | Second Spin | Outcome |
|------------|-------------|---------|
| blue | blue | blue-blue |
| | yellow | blue-yellow |
| yellow | blue | yellow-blue |
| | yellow | yellow-yellow |

A carnival committee is considering using the Red and Blue game. The game involves choosing one marble at random from each of two buckets. The first bucket contains one green, one blue, one red, and one yellow marble. The second bucket contains one green, one red, and one yellow marble.

Without looking, a player chooses one marble from each bucket in the Red and Blue game. If the player gets a red and a blue marble (the order makes no difference), the player wins. Each player pays $1 to play and receives $3 for each win.

**Bucket 1**             **Bucket 2**

**A.** Before playing the game, do you predict that the school will make money on this game? Explain.

**B.** Make a tree diagram to show the possible outcomes for this game. Explain how your tree shows all the possible outcomes.

**C.** What is the theoretical probability of choosing a red and blue marble on a turn?

**D.** Suppose the game is played 36 times.

  **1.** How much money can the school expect to collect?

  **2.** How much money can the school expect to pay out to the winners?

  **3.** Did the school make money? If so, how much?

**E.** Suppose one marble is chosen from each bucket. Find the probability of each situation.

  **1.** You choose a green marble from Bucket 1 and a yellow marble from Bucket 2.

  **2.** You do *not* choose a blue marble from either bucket.

  **3.** You choose two blue marbles.

  **4.** You choose at least one blue marble.

**ACE** **Homework starts on page 10.**

# 1.3 Playing the Multiplication Game

You have played games that use the sum of two number cubes. In the following game, scoring depends on the *product* of the numbers rolled.

## Problem 1.3 Determining Whether a Game Is Fair

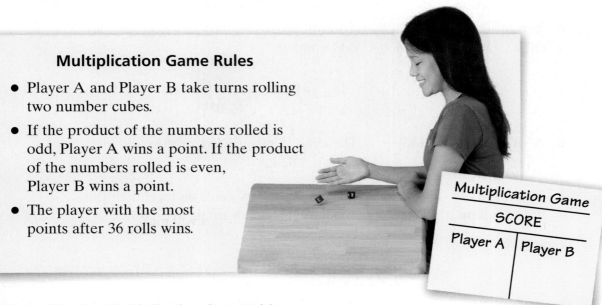

**Multiplication Game Rules**

- Player A and Player B take turns rolling two number cubes.
- If the product of the numbers rolled is odd, Player A wins a point. If the product of the numbers rolled is even, Player B wins a point.
- The player with the most points after 36 rolls wins.

Multiplication Game
SCORE

| Player A | Player B |
| --- | --- |
|  |  |

**A. 1.** Play the Multiplication Game with a partner for a total of 36 turns. Keep track of your results.

**2.** Based on your data, what is the experimental probability of rolling an odd product? What is the probability of an even product?

**B. 1.** List the possible products. In how many different ways can each product occur?

**2.** Is each product equally likely? Explain.

**3.** What is the theoretical probability of rolling an odd product? What is the theoretical probability of rolling an even product?

**C.** Suppose the game has 100 rolls instead of 36. How many points do you expect each player to have at the end of the game?

**D.** Do you think the Multiplication Game is fair? Explain. If the game is not fair, explain how the rules could be changed so that the game is fair.

**ACE** Homework starts on page 10.

## Applications

**1.** Decide whether the possible resulting events are equally likely. Explain.

| **Action** | **Possible resulting events** |
|---|---|
| **a.** You roll a number cube. | You roll an even number, or you roll an odd number. |

| | |
|---|---|
| **b.** A young child grows. | The child is left-handed, or the child is right-handed. |
| **c.** You toss a marshmallow. | The marshmallow lands on its end, or the marshmallow lands on its curved side. |

| | |
|---|---|
| **d.** You choose a card from a standard deck of 52 playing cards with no jokers. | The card is a heart, the card is a club, the card is a diamond, or the card is a spade. |
| **e.** You toss a coin three times. | You get three heads, two heads and a tail, a head and two tails, or three tails. |

**2.** Lori's little sister Emily tore the labels from ten cans of vegetables. Now all the cans look exactly the same. Three cans are corn, two are spinach, four are beans, and one is tomatoes. Lori picks a can at random. Find each probability.

Go Online
PHSchool.com

**For:** Multiple-Choice Skills
Practice
**Web Code:** ana-7154

**a.** *P*(corn)  **b.** *P*(beans)

**c.** *P*(not spinach)  **d.** *P*(beans or tomatoes)

**e.** Is each vegetable equally likely to be in the can? Explain.

3. Jacob has a probability party. He serves three items, each item selected at random from two options. Each guest gets a hamburger or a hot dog, cole slaw or potato salad, and an apple or an orange.

   a. Make a tree diagram to show all possibilities.

   b. What is the probability that Samantha gets a hot dog, cole slaw, and an orange?

   c. Rick does not like hot dogs. What is the probability that he will *not* be served a hot dog?

4. José is going to a party. He decides to wear his jeans and a sweater, but he hasn't decided what else to wear. The tree diagram shows the possible outfits he can make if he chooses sneakers or loafers; a pair of blue, red, or white socks; and a green, red, or plaid cap, at random.

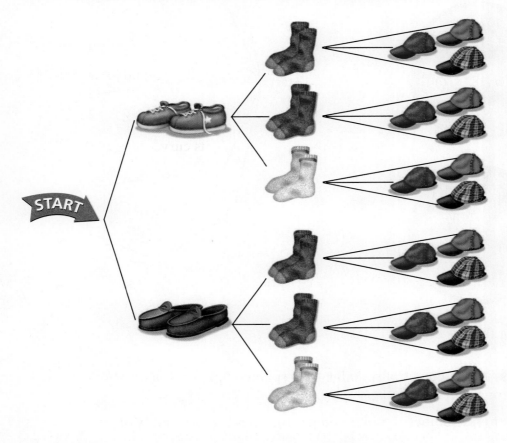

   a. What is the probability that José will wear loafers, blue socks, and a plaid cap?

   b. What is the probability that José will wear sneakers, either red or blue socks, and a green cap?

   c. What is the probability that José will wear neither red socks nor a red cap?

**For Exercises 5–9, Monita and Kyan are analyzing a game involving two different spinners. A turn is one spin on each spinner. They make this tree diagram of equally likely outcomes to find theoretical probabilities.**

**5. Multiple Choice** Choose the spinner that could be Spinner X.

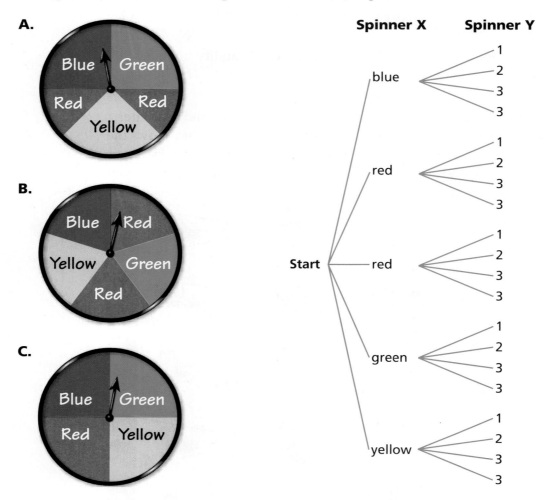

**A.**

**B.**

**C.**

**D.** None of these is correct.

**6.** List all possible outcomes of spinning each spinner, Spinner X and Spinner Y, once.

**7.** Which color and number combination has the greatest probability of occurring?

**8.** What is the probability of getting red on Spinner X and 3 on Spinner Y?

**9.** What is the probability of *not* getting a 3 on Spinner Y?

**10.** In the Gee Whiz Everyone Wins! game show, members of the audience choose a block at random from the bucket shown at the right. If a blue block is chosen, the contestant wins $5. If a red block is chosen, the contestant wins $10. If the yellow block is chosen, the contestant wins $50. The block is replaced after each turn.

    **a.** What is the probability of choosing each color? Explain your method.

    **b.** Suppose 24 contestants choose and replace a block. How much money can the game show expect to pay out?

**11.** In Raymundo's Prime Number Multiplication Game, a player rolls two number cubes. Player A gets 10 points if the product is prime. Player B gets 1 point if the product is not prime. Raymundo thinks this scoring system is reasonable because there are many more ways to roll a non-prime product than a prime product.

    **a.** If the cubes are rolled 100 times, how many points would you expect Player A to score? How many points would you expect Player B to score?

    **b.** Is Raymundo's game a fair game? Explain.

**12.** Rachel says that if she rolls two number cubes 36 times, she will get a product of 1 exactly once. Mariana said that she cannot be sure this will happen exactly once, but it will probably happen very few times. Who is right? Explain your reasoning.

**13.** Rachel told Mariana that if she rolls two number cubes 100 times, she will never get a product of 23. Mariana told her that she can't be sure. Who is right? Explain.

# Connections

**14.** The probability of an event is a number between 0 (0%) and 1 (100%). The larger the probability, the greater the chances the event will occur. If an event is impossible, the probability that it will occur is 0 (or 0%). If an event is certain to happen, the probability that it will occur is 1, or 100%.

Copy the scale below. Place the letter of each event a–i on the scale at the spot that best describes its probability.

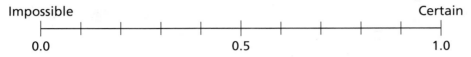

Impossible                               Certain

0.0                        0.5                     1.0

**a.** You get a head when you toss a coin.

**b.** You run 20 miles in one hour.

**c.** You roll a 6 on a number cube.

**d.** Your neighbor's cat has four legs.

**e.** The sun will rise tomorrow.

**f.** You toss a coin twice and get two heads.

**g.** You toss a coin twice and get at least one head.

**h.** You listen to a CD today.

**i.** You spin the spinner below, and it lands on red.

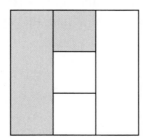

**15.** **Multiple Choice** What fraction of this diagram is shaded?

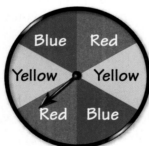

**F.** $\frac{1}{2}$          **G.** $\frac{2}{5}$          **H.** $\frac{1}{3}$          **J.** $\frac{4}{9}$

**Homework Help Online**
PHSchool.com

**For:** Help with Exercise 15
**Web Code:** ane-7115

**16.** Write three fractions equivalent to the fraction you chose in Exercise 15.

**17. Multiple Choice** What fraction of this diagram is shaded?

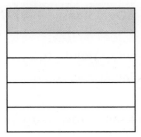

**A.** $\frac{20}{100}$ **B.** $\frac{4}{8}$ **C.** $\frac{1}{2}$ **D.** $\frac{1}{4}$

**18.** Write three fractions equivalent to the fraction you chose in Exercise 17.

**19.** Fala spins this spinner several times. The table shows the results.

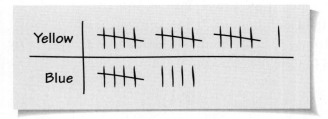

a. How many times did Fala spin the spinner?

b. What percent of the spins landed in the blue region? What percent landed in the yellow region?

c. According to the theoretical probabilities, what is the percent of the spins expected to land in the blue region over the long run? In the yellow region?

d. Compare the experimental probability of the spinner landing in each region with the theoretical probability. If the probabilities are different, explain why.

**20.** If you drop a tack on the floor, there are two possible outcomes: the tack lands on its side (point down), or the tack lands on its head (point up). Kalifa dropped a tack 100 times. The table shows the results.

point down          point up

| Outcomes | Number of Times It Occurs |
|---|---|
| Tack lands point up | 58 |
| Tack lands point down | 42 |

**a.** Suppose you drop Kalifa's tack 500 times. How many times do you expect it to land point up?

**b.** Is it equally likely that the tack will land point up or point down? Explain.

**c.** Is it possible to determine theoretical probabilities for this situation? Why or why not?

**21.** Juanita is deciding whether to play a game at an amusement park. It takes one ticket to play the game. A player tosses two plastic bottles. If both bottles land standing up, the player wins ten tickets to use for rides and games. Juanita watches people play and records the results.

| Both land on side | One lands on side and one lands standing up | Both land standing up |
|---|---|---|
| ⵌⵌ ⵌⵌ ⵌⵌ ⵌⵌ ‖‖‖‖ | ⵌⵌ ⵌⵌ ‖‖‖‖ | ‖‖ |

**a.** Based on Juanita's results, what is the experimental probability of winning the game?

**b.** Suppose Juanita plays this game 20 times. How many times can she expect to win?

**c.** How many tickets can Juanita expect to be ahead or behind after playing the game 20 times? Explain your reasoning.

**d.** Is it possible to find the theoretical probability of winning this game? Why or why not?

**22.** A bucket contains 60 marbles. Some are red, some are blue, and some are white. The probability of drawing a red marble is 35%. The probability of drawing a blue marble is 25%. How many marbles of each color are in the bucket?

**23.** Hannah's teacher brought in a bucket containing 72 blocks. The blocks are red, yellow, or blue. Hannah wants to figure out the number of blue blocks without emptying the bucket.

Hannah chooses a block from the bucket, records its color, and then replaces it. Of her 14 draws, she records blue 5 times. Based on Hannah's experiment, how many of the blocks are blue? Explain.

**24.** Suppose you roll two number cubes. What is the probability that the product of the numbers will be a multiple of 5?

**25.** If you roll two number cubes 100 times, about how many times can you expect the product of the numbers to be a multiple of 5?

**26.** Suppose you roll two number cubes. What is the probability that the product of the numbers is a multiple of 7?

**27.** If you roll two number cubes a million times, about how many times can you expect the product of the numbers to be a multiple of 7?

**28.** Suppose you roll two number cubes and multiply the numbers. Find each probability.

**a.** $P$(product is a multiple of 3 and 4)

**b.** $P$(product is a multiple of 3 or 4)

**c.** $P$(product has a factor of 5 and 3)

**d.** $P$(product is a prime number)

**e.** $P$(product is greater than 10)

**f.** $P$(product is less than 18)

# Extensions

**29.** Tricia wants to determine the probability of getting two 1's when two number cubes are rolled. She makes a tree diagram and uses it to list the possible outcomes.

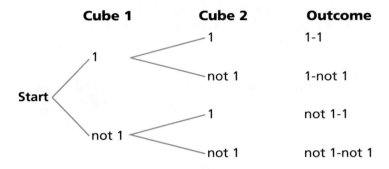

She says that, because there are four possible outcomes, the probability of getting 1 on both number cubes is $\frac{1}{4}$. Is Tricia right? Explain.

**30.** Juan invented a two-person game in which players take turns rolling three number cubes. If the sum is even, Player A gets a point. If the sum is odd, Player B gets a point. Is Juan's game a fair game? Explain.

**For Exercises 31–33, a computer places a dot at random on each dartboard below.**

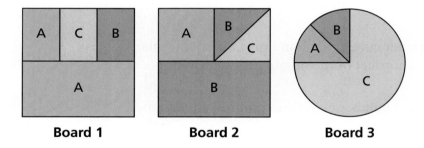

Board 1          Board 2          Board 3

**31.** For each dartboard, what is the probability that a dot will be in a region marked A? A region marked B? A region marked C?

**32.** For Board 1, what is the probability that a dot will be in a region marked A or B?

**33.** For Board 2, what is the probability that a dot will *not* be in region C?

# Mathematical Reflections 1

**I**n this investigation, you explored games of chance. Working on the problems gave you an opportunity to review ideas about experimental and theoretical probability. The following questions will help you summarize what you have learned.

Think about your answers to these questions. Discuss your ideas with other students and your teacher. Then write a summary of your findings in your notebook.

1. **a.** Compare experimental and theoretical probabilities.

   **b.** Describe some strategies you can use to find experimental probabilities.

   **c.** Describe some strategies you can use to find theoretical probabilities.

2. How do you use probabilities, either theoretical or experimental, to decide if a particular game of chance is fair?

3. In a game of chance, how can you predict the number of times out of 100 a given outcome will occur?

# Analyzing Situations Using an Area Model

**E**ach turn in the games of chance in the last Investigation involved two actions. For example, in the spinner game, you spun the pointer twice and then determined the outcome. You determined the theoretical probabilities of these games using a variety of strategies.

In this Investigation, you will learn how to use an area model to analyze probability situations that involve more than one action on a turn. You can analyze games such as the Red and Blue game in Problem 1.2 using an **area model.**

Bucket 1 contains three marbles—one red and two greens. Bucket 2 contains four marbles—one red, one blue, one green, and one yellow.

**Bucket 1**

**Bucket 2**

- Draw a square on grid paper. Suppose the square has an area of 1 square unit. We use the square to represent a probability of 1.

Bucket 2

Bucket 1

- The first bucket has three equally likely choices: red, green, and the other green. Divide the square into three sections with equal areas. The areas of the sections represent the probabilities of the three choices. Label the sections.

- For the second action of choosing a marble from Bucket 2, subdivide the diagram to represent the probabilities of the equally likely choices: red, blue, green, and yellow. Label these new Bucket 2 sections.

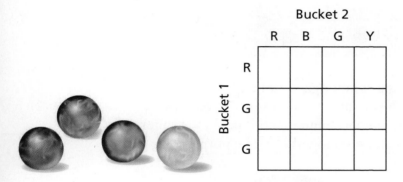

- Each subregion formed represents one of the outcomes: RR, RB, RG, RY, GR, GB, GG, and GY.

**Bucket 2**

| | | R | B | G | Y |
|---|---|---|---|---|---|
| **Bucket 1** | R | RR | RB | RG | RY |
| | G | GR | GB | GG | GY |
| | G | GR | GB | GG | GY |

- The area of each subregion represents the probability for each outcome.

*What is the probability of choosing an RR? RB? RG? RY? GR? GB? GG? GY? YY?*

*What is the probability of choosing a red from either bucket?*

A popular game at a school carnival is a spinner game called Making Purple. To play the game, a player spins the pointer of each spinner below once. Suppose a player gets red on one spinner and blue on the other spinner. The player wins, because red and blue together make purple.

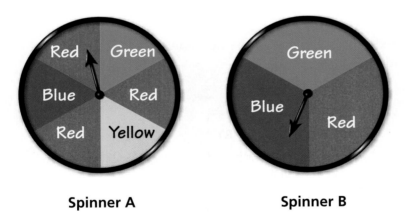

Spinner A                    Spinner B

**A.** Play the Making Purple game several times. Record the results of each turn. Based on your results, what is the experimental probability that a player will "make purple" on a turn?

**B.** Use an area model to determine the theoretical probability that a player will make purple on a turn.

**C.** How does the experimental probability of making purple compare with the theoretical probability of making purple?

**D.** The cost to play the game is $2. The winner gets $6 for making purple. Suppose 36 people play the game.

   **1.** How much money will the school take in from this game?

   **2.** How much money do you expect the school to pay out in prizes?

   **3.** How much profit do you expect the school to make from this game?

ACE **Homework starts on page 27.**

**Choosing Paths**

**K**enisha is designing a game involving paths through the woods that lead to caves. Before the game is played the player chooses either Cave A or Cave B. Next, the player starts at the beginning and chooses a path at random at each fork. If the player lands in the cave that was chosen in the beginning, he or she wins a prize.

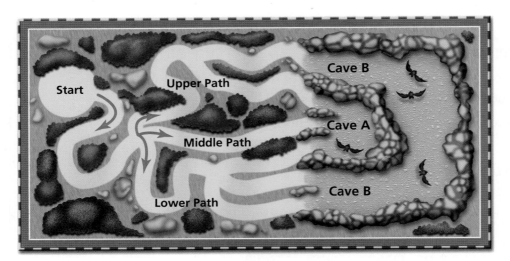

**Getting Ready for Problem** 2.2

- Are you more likely to end in Cave A or in Cave B? Why?

The 18 students in Sarah's class design an experiment to find the likelihood of ending in Cave A or in Cave B. For each trial, they trace the path beginning at Start, and use a number cube to make the choice of direction whenever there is a split in the path.

- Is this a good way to find the experimental probability of the game? Explain.

- Are there other ways to make choices at a split in the path? Explain.

**A.** Carry out the experiment to simulate the 18 students playing the game and note the cave where each student ends.

**B.** What is the experimental probability of landing in Cave A? Of landing in Cave B?

**C.** Miguel draws this diagram to help him find the theoretical probabilities of ending in Cave A or in Cave B.

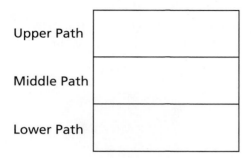

1. Explain what Miguel has done so far. Does this look reasonable?

2. Complete an area model to find the theoretical probabilities of ending in Cave A or Cave B. Show your work.

**D.** How are your experimental probabilities from Question A related to the theoretical probabilities?

**E.** Kenisha designs a new version of the game. It has a different arrangement of paths leading to Caves A and B. She makes the area model below to analyze the probabilities of ending in each cave.

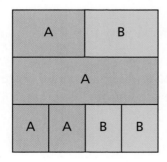

1. Create a path game that fits the model.

2. Find the probability for each outcome.

ACE **Homework starts on page 27.**

Brianna and Emmanuel are chosen from the studio audience of the Gee Whiz Everyone Wins! game show to play a game. While Emmanuel waits backstage, Brianna places two green marbles and two blue marbles in two identical containers in any arrangement she chooses.

After she places the marbles, Emmanuel returns. He chooses one of the containers at random. He then chooses a marble from that container without looking. If he chooses a green marble, the friends each win a prize. If he chooses a blue marble, or if the container he chooses is empty, the friends do not win anything.

**Problem 2.3 Finding the Best Arrangement**

**A.** List all the different ways Brianna can place the four marbles in the two containers.

**B.** For each arrangement, what is the probability that Emmanuel chooses a green marble?

**C.** Which arrangement will give Brianna and Emmanuel the greatest chance of winning? The least chance of winning? Explain.

ACE Homework starts on page 27.

## Applications

1. Bonita and Deion are using the spinners from the Making Purple game in Problem 2.1. They take turns spinning. If the colors on the two spinners make purple, Deion scores. If they do not make purple, Bonita scores. For this to be a fair game, how many points should Deion score when the spinners make purple, and how many points should Bonita score when they do not make purple?

2. At the Flag Day Festival at Parker Middle School, there is a contest where a player chooses one block from each of two different bags. A player wins if he or she picks a red and a blue block. James makes the tree diagram below to find the probability of winning.

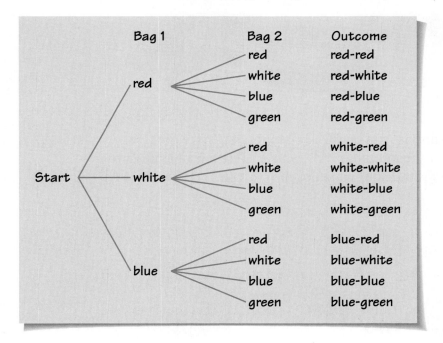

   a. What blocks are in bag 1?
   b. What blocks are in bag 2?
   c. Draw an area model that represents this contest.
   d. What is the probability of winning this contest?

**Go Online**
PHSchool.com

**For:** Multiple-Choice Skills Practice
**Web Code:** ana-7254

3. There are two No-Cavity prize bins at a dentist's office. One bin has two hot-pink toothbrushes and three neon-yellow toothbrushes. The other bin has four packs of sugar-free gum, three grape and one strawberry. Kira has no cavities. The dentist tells her to close her eyes and choose a prize from each bin.

   **a.** What is the probability that Kira will choose a neon-yellow toothbrush and a pack of sugar-free grape gum? Draw an area model to support your solution.

   **b.** The dental assistant refills the bins after every patient. Suppose the next 100 patients have no cavities. How many times do you expect the patients to get the same prizes that Kira chose?

4. Al is about to ski his last run on Morey Mountain. There are five trails to the base of the mountain. Al wants to take a trail leading to the lodge. He can't remember which trail(s) to take.

Morey Mountain

Ski Lift          Lodge          Ski Shop

   **a.** Design an experiment using a number cube to find the experimental probability of Al ending at the lodge. Conduct the experiment 20 times. If you do not have a number cube, write the numbers 1–6 on pieces of paper. Then select one from a hat.

**b.** What is the experimental probability of Al ending at the lodge? At the lift? At the ski shop?

**c.** Find the theoretical probability of ending at the lodge, the lift, and the ski shop. Compare the experimental and theoretical probabilities. Do you have more confidence in the experimental or the theoretical probability? Why?

**5.** Kenisha changes the game in Problem 2.2 so it has the paths below.

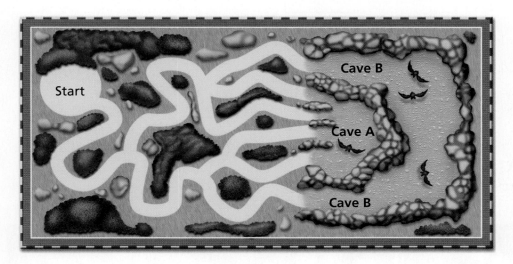

**a.** Suppose a player chooses a path at random at each fork. What is the theoretical probability that he or she will end in Cave A? In Cave B? Show your work.

**b.** If you play this game 100 times, how many times do you expect to end in Cave A? In Cave B?

**6.** Kenisha designs another version of the game in Problem 2.2. The new version has a different arrangement of paths leading into Caves A and B. She makes an area model to analyze the probabilities of landing in each cave.

For Kenisha's new version, what is the probability that a player will end in Cave A? In Cave B?

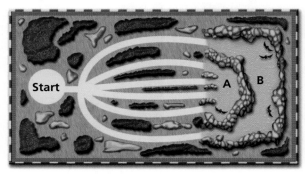

**7. Multiple Choice** Choose the map that the area model in Exercise 6 could represent.

**A.**

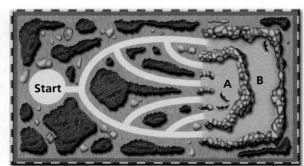

**B.**

**C.**

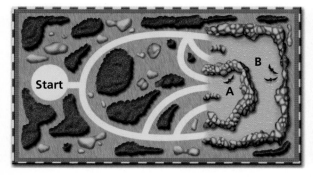

**D.**

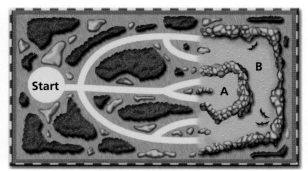

For Exercises 8–10, suppose a bag contains three orange marbles and two blue marbles. You are to choose a marble, return it to the bag, and then choose again.

**8.** Choose an appropriate method from those below for finding the possible outcomes. Describe how you would use your choice.

   **a.** make a tree diagram

   **b.** make a list

   **c.** use an area model

   **d.** make a table or chart

**9.** Suppose you do this experiment 50 times. Use the method you chose in Exercise 8 to predict the number of times you will choose two marbles of the same color.

**10.** Suppose this experiment is a two-person game in which one player scores if the marbles match, and the other player scores if they do not match. Suppose the two players play the game many times and total the points scored. Describe a scoring system that makes this a game in which each person has an equally likely chance of having the winning score.

Brianna (from Problem 2.3) is given each set of marbles to distribute between two containers. What arrangement gives Emmanuel the best chance of choosing a green marble?

**11.** three blue and two green marbles

**12.** two blue and three green marbles

# Connections

**13.** In a survey, 100 seniors at a high school were asked these questions:

- Do you favor a rule that allows only seniors to drive to school?

- Do you drive to school?

**Homework Help Online**
PHSchool.com

**For:** Help with Exercise 13
**Web Code:** ane-7213

### Driving Survey

|  | Drives to School | Does Not Drive to School | Row Totals |
|---|---|---|---|
| **Favors Rule** | 40 | 30 | 70 |
| **Opposes Rule** | 20 | 10 | 30 |
| **Total** | 60 | 40 | 100 |

**a.** Based on this survey, what is the probability that a senior chosen at random favors the rule?

**b.** What is the probability that a senior chosen at random drives to school and favors the rule?

**c.** What is the probability that a senior chosen at random drives to school or opposes the rule?

**d.** Are the results of this survey a good indicator of how all the students at the high school feel about the driving rule? Explain.

**14.** Marni and Ira are playing a game with this square spinner. A game is 10 turns. Each turn is 2 spins. The numbers for the 2 spins are added. Marni scores 1 point for a sum that is negative, and Ira scores 1 point for a sum that is positive. After 10 turns, each player totals their points. The one with more points wins.

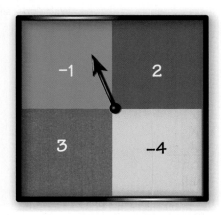

  **a.** List all of the possible outcomes.

  **b.** Are Marni and Ira equally likely to win?

**Megan is designing a computer game called *Treasure Hunt*. The computer chooses a square at random on the grid at the right, and then hides a treasure in the room containing that square. For Exercises 15–19, use the grid to find the probability that the computer will hide the treasure in each room.**

**15.** Library

**16.** Den

**17.** Dining hall

**18.** Great hall

**19.** Front hall

**20. Multiple Choice** Megan enlarges the floor plan in the game grid above by a scale factor of 2. How does this affect the probabilities that the treasure is in each room?

  **F.** They are unchanged.

  **G.** They are $\frac{1}{2}$ the original probability.

  **H.** They are twice the original.

  **J.** They are four times the original.

**21.** Carlos is also designing a *Treasure Hunt* game. He keeps track of the number of times the computer hides the treasure in each room. Here is a line plot of his results.

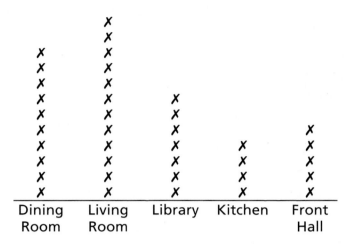

Design a floor plan that could give this data. State the area of each room on your floor plan.

**22.** Fergus designs a dartboard for a school carnival. His design is shown below. He must decide how much to charge a player and how much to pay out for a win. To do this, he needs to know the probabilities of landing in sections marked A and B. Assume the darts land at random on the dartboard.

**a.** What is the probability of landing in a section marked A?

**b.** What is the probability of landing in a section marked B?

**23.** Fergus designs two more dartboards for the school carnival.

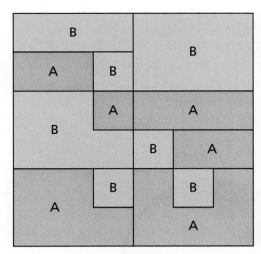

Dartboard 1          Dartboard 2

**a.** What is the probability of landing in sections marked A on Dartboard 1? On Dartboard 2? Explain.

**b.** A player pays $1 to play and wins $2 if the dart lands in sections marked B. If the dart lands in sections marked A, the player wins no money.

   **i.** How much money will the player expect to make (or lose) after 36 turns using Dartboard 1? Using Dartboard 2? Explain.

   **ii.** How much money will the carnival expect to make (or lose) after 36 turns using Dartboard 1? Using Dartboard 2?

**c.** Can the carnival expect to make a profit on this game with either board? Explain.

**24. a.** If you roll one number cube two times, what is the probability of getting a factor of 5 both times?

**b.** Suppose you roll two different number cubes. What is the probability of getting a factor of 5 on both cubes?

**c.** How do your answers to parts (a) and (b) compare? Explain why the answers have this relationship.

Connections

# Extensions

**25.** Suppose you play a game using the two spinners below. You get two spins. You may spin each spinner once, or you may spin one of the spinners twice. If you get a red on one spin and a blue on the other spin (the order makes no difference), you win. To have the greatest chance of winning, should you spin Spinner A twice, spin Spinner B twice, or spin each spinner once? Explain.

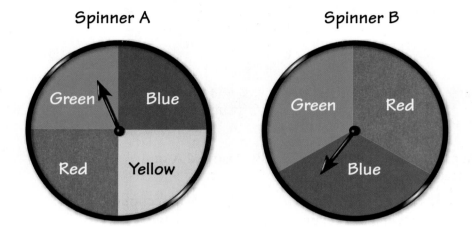

**26.** Suppose Brianna (from Problem 2.3) is given two green marbles, two blue marbles, and three buckets. How can she put the marbles in the three buckets to have the best chance of choosing a green marble?

**27.** Della is chosen as a contestant on a game show. The host gives her two red marbles, two green marbles, and two yellow marbles.

Della will put the marbles into two identical cans in any way she chooses. The host will then rearrange the cans, leaving the marbles as Della placed them. Della will then select a can and choose a marble. If she chooses a red marble, she wins a prize.

How should Della arrange the marbles so she has the best chance of choosing a red marble?

**28.** Make up your own marbles and buckets problem. Find the solution.

# Mathematical Reflections 2

**I**n this investigation, you analyzed probabilities of two-stage events by dividing the area of a square. The following questions will help you summarize what you have learned.

Think about your answers to these questions. Discuss your ideas with other students and your teacher. Then write a summary of your findings in your notebook.

1. Describe three or four probability situations that involve two actions. Describe the outcomes for these situations.

2. Describe how you can use an area model to determine the probability of a situation that involves two actions.

# Investigation 3

## Expected Value

**O**n April 14, 1993, during halftime of a basketball game between the Chicago Bulls and the Miami Heat, Don Calhoun won $1 million by making a basket from the free-throw line at the opposite end of the court. Don was chosen at random to attempt the basket as part of a promotional contest. A *Sports Illustrated* article explained:

> *The odds against one randomly chosen person given one shot from the opposite foul line and making it are considered astronomical. Scottie Pippen admitted that after practice one day he and Michael Jordan tried to hit the shot but couldn't.*
>
> (Source: Bessone, Lisa, "Sports People: Don Calhoun." *Sports Illustrated*, April 26, 1993, vol 48.)

Fortunately, not every basket is this difficult to make! In this Investigation, you will use a player's free-throw percent to figure out what is likely to happen in a given free-throw situation.

### 3.1 One-and-One Free-Throws

**I**n the district finals, Nishi's basketball team is 1 point behind with 2 seconds left. Nishi has just been fouled, and she is in a one-and-one free-throw situation. This means that Nishi will try one free throw. If she makes it, she tries a second free throw. If she misses the first time, she does not get a second try. Nishi's free-throw average is 60%.

- What are the possible scores Nishi can make in a one-and-one free-throw situation?
- How can each score be made?
- How would you design an experiment to analyze this situation?

---

## Problem **3.1** Simulating a Probability Situation

**A.** Is it most likely that Nishi will score 0 points, 1 point, or 2 points? Record what you think before you analyze the situation.

**B.** Use this spinner to simulate Nishi's one-and-one situation 20 times. Record the result of each trial.

**C.** Based on your results, what is the experimental probability that Nishi will score 0 points? That she will score 1 point? That she will score 2 points?

**D.** Make an area model for this situation using a 10 × 10 grid. What is the theoretical probability that Nishi will score 0 points? That she will score 1 point? That she will score 2 points? Compare the three theoretical probabilities with the three experimental probabilities.

**E.** Suppose Nishi's free-throw average is 70%. How does this affect the outcome? Explain.

**F.** How does the diagram in Question D help you predict how many times Nishi will score 2 points in 100 one-and-one situations? In 200 one-and-one situations?

ACE Homework starts on page 43.

# 3.2 Finding Expected Value

In Problem 3.1, you looked at the probabilities of different outcomes of Nishi's one-and-one free-throw situation. You might have been surprised about which outcome is most likely. In this Problem, you will look at the number of points Nishi can expect to make each time she is in a one-and-one free-throw situation.

## Problem 3.2 Finding Expected Value

Suppose Nishi has a 60% free-throw percentage and is in a one-and-one free-throw situation 100 times during the season.

**A.** **1.** How many times can she expect to score 0 points? What is the total number of points for these situations?

   **2.** How many times can she expect to score 1 point? What is the total number of points for these situations?

   **3.** How many times can she expect to score 2 points? What is the total number of points for these situations?

   **4.** What total number of points do you expect Nishi to score in these 100 situations at the free-throw line?

   **5.** What would Nishi's average number of points (expected value) per situation be?

**B. 1.** In a one-and-one situation, what score is most likely to happen for a player whose free-throw percentage is 20%? 40%? 60%? 80%?

**2.** Copy and complete the table at the right for the players in part (1) in 100 one-and-one situations. You will fill in the expected value column in part (3).

**3.** Calculate the average number of points for each situation. Record these values in the table in part (2). Describe any pattern you see.

**Points Expected in 100 One-and-One Situations**

| Player's Free-Throw Percentage | Points | | | |
|---|---|---|---|---|
| | 0 | 1 | 2 | Expected Value, or Average |
| 20% | ■ | ■ | ■ | ■ |
| 40% | ■ | ■ | ■ | ■ |
| 60% | ■ | ■ | ■ | ■ |
| 80% | ■ | ■ | ■ | ■ |

**C. 1.** Make a graph like the one started at the right for each of the players in your table. Use your graph to answer parts (2)–(4).

**2.** How does the average number of points compare for players with a 20% free-throw percentage, a 40% free-throw percentage, a 60% free-throw percentage, and an 80% free-throw percentage?

**3.** Nishi's dad noticed that he makes an average of about 1 point in one-and-one free-throw situations. What is his free-throw percentage?

**4.** Nishi's older sister has a 70% free-throw percentage. What is her average number of points in one-and-one situations? Check your answer by making an area model.

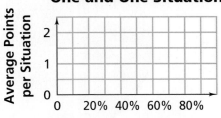

**Points Expected in a One-and-One Situation**

**ACE** Homework starts on page 43.

## 3.3 Choosing Pay Plans

The average number of points in the one-and-one situation is the **expected value** for this situation. Expected value is used in a variety of other situations such as determining life-insurance premiums and lottery prizes, and for predicting gains and losses in businesses. The following problem shows another situation in which expected value is useful.

Julie and Brandon cut lawns for their neighbors to earn money to donate to a local charity. They thought that customers should pay $20. However, several customers offered a different pay plan and asked the students to choose. Julie and Brandon have to decide which of the pay plans would give them a fair deal over the long run.

In each case, calculate the expected value. Then, decide whether they should accept or reject the pay plan. Give reasons for your decision.

**A.** The customer spins each of these spinners once. If one spinner is red and the other is blue (the order makes no difference), Julie and Brandon get $24. Otherwise, they get $10.

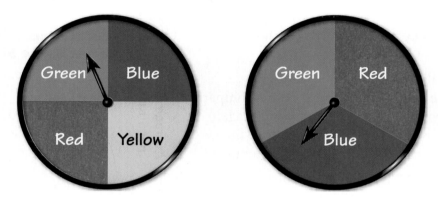

**B.** The customer rolls a pair of number cubes and adds the two numbers. If the sum is even, Julie and Brandon get $25. If it is odd, they get $18.

**C.** The customer rolls a pair of number cubes. If the product is 24, Julie and Brandon get $40. Otherwise, they get $10.

**D.** The customer places a twenty-dollar bill and three one-dollar bills in a bag. Julie and Brandon choose two bills. The money they choose is their payment.

**E.** The customer tosses three coins. If two or more land heads up, Julie and Brandon get $25. Otherwise, they get $15.

ACE | **Homework starts on page 43.**

## Applications

In a one-and-one free-throw situation, is the player with each free-throw average most likely to score 0 points, 1 point, or 2 points? Make an area model to support each answer.

**1.** an 80% average

**2.** a 40% average

For Exercises 3–5, use the information in the table. It shows statistics for some of the players on a basketball team.

**Free-Throw Statistics**

| Name | Free Throws Attempted | Free Throws Made |
|------|----------------------|------------------|
| Gerrit | 54 | 27 |
| David | 49 | 39 |
| Ken | 73 | 45 |
| Alex | 60 | 42 |

**3. a.** Which player has the best chance of making his next free throw? Explain your reasoning.

  **b.** What is the free-throw probability for each player?

**4. a.** Alex has just been fouled and is in a one-and-one free-throw situation. What is the probability he will score 0 points? 1 point? 2 points?

  **b.** Suppose Alex is in a one-and-one situation 100 times. How many times do you expect each of the outcomes in part (a) to occur?

  **c.** What is the average number of points you expect Alex to make in a one-and-one situation?

  **d.** Repeat part (a) using Gerrit.

**5. a.** In a different type of free-throw situation, a player gets a second attempt, even if the first free-throw is missed. Suppose Gerrit is in this two-attempt free-throw situation. What is the probability he will score 0 points? 1 point? 2 points?

  **b.** Compare your answers to part (a) with Exercise 4(d). Explain why the answers are not exactly the same.

**Homework**
**Help** Online
PHSchool.com
**For:** Help with Exercise 6
**Web Code:** ane-7306

**6.** Nishi, who has a 60% free-throw average, is in a two-attempt free-throw situation. Remember, this means that she will attempt the second free-throw no matter what happens on the first.

   **a.** Is Nishi most likely to score 0 points, 1 point, or 2 points? Explain.

   **b.** Nishi plans to keep track of her score on two-attempt free-throw situations. What average number of points can she expect to score in two-attempt situations?

**7.** Repeat Exercise 6 for the player with each free-throw average.

   **a.** a 50% average          **b.** an 80% average

**8.** In each of the following situations, the customer should pay $10 per week for newspapers. Drew, the paper carrier, has to decide which customer suggestions give him a fair deal over the long run. In each case, decide if Drew should accept or reject his customer's suggestion.

   **a.** The customer puts a ten-dollar bill and two one-dollar bills in a bag. Drew chooses two bills.

   **b.** Drew tosses three coins. If they are all heads or all tails, Drew gets $30. Otherwise, he gets $2.

   **c.** Drew rolls a pair of number cubes. If the sum is 7, Drew gets $50. Otherwise, he gets $2.

# Connections

A game show uses a large spinner with many sections. At least one section is labeled "bankrupt." If a player spins "bankrupt," he or she loses that turn and all his or her money. Carlota makes a version of the spinner at the right.

**9.** What is the probability that a player who spins the spinner one time will land on bankrupt?

**10.** What is the probability that a player who spins the spinner one time will get $500 or more?

**11.** Sam just spun the spinner and it landed on $350. What is the probability he will land on $350 on his next spin? Explain your reasoning.

**Multiple Choice** For Exercises 12–14, choose the answer that is the correct percent of the given number.

**12.** 30% of 90

   **A.** 60       **B.** 27       **C.** 30       **D.** 3

**13.** 25% of 80

   **F.** 20       **G.** 3.2       **H.** 0.3175       **J.** 200

**14.** 45% of 180

   **A.** 2.5       **B.** 40       **C.** 81       **D.** 4

**Go Online**
PHSchool.com

**For:** Multiple-Choice Skills Practice
**Web Code:** ana-7354

**15.** Wanda, the Channel 1 weather person, said there was a 30% chance of rain on Saturday and a 30% chance of rain on Sunday. It rained both days, and Wanda's station manager is wondering if she should fire Wanda.

   **a.** Suppose Wanda's calculations were correct and there was a 30% chance of rain each day. What was the probability that there would be rain on both days?

   **b.** Do you think Wanda should be fired? Why or why not?

   **c.** Wanda is working on her predictions for the next few days. She calculates that there is a 20% chance of rain on Monday and a 20% chance of rain on Tuesday. If she is correct, what is the probability that it will rain on at least one of these days?

**16.** A lake has 10,000 fish. When a fisherman scoops up his net, he catches 500 fish. Suppose 150 of the 500 fish in his net are salmon. How many salmon do you predict are in the lake?

**17. a.** Copy the table below. Use your answers from Problem 3.2, Question C to fill in your table.

| Probability of One Basket | 20% | 40% | 60% | 80% | 100% |
|---|---|---|---|---|---|
| Average Points per One-and-One Attempt | 0.24 | ▨ | 0.96 | ▨ | ▨ |

**b.** Is the average for 80% twice that of 40%?

**c.** Use this table or your graph from Problem 3.2, Question C. Is the average for 100% twice the average of 50%?

**d.** A player with a 20% free-throw average makes 0.24 points, on average, in a one-and-one situation. Copy and complete this table. How are the relationships in this table different from the table in part (a)?

| Number of One-and-One Situations by a Player With a 20% Average | 1 | 10 | 20 | 100 |
|---|---|---|---|---|
| Average Points Made | 0.24 | ▨ | ▨ | ▨ |

**For Exercises 18 and 19, spin each spinner once. Use the spinners below.**

**18.** Suppose you add the results.

**a.** What is the probability of getting a positive number?

**b.** What is the average value?

**19.** Suppose you multiply the results.

**a.** What is the probability of getting a positive number?

**b.** What is the average value?

**20.** Fred and Joseph are experimenting with a new game. The probability Fred wins a round of this game is $\frac{1}{3}$ and the probability Joseph wins a round is $\frac{2}{3}$. They decide that to make the game fair, Fred scores 3 points when he wins a round, and Joseph scores 2 points when he wins a round.

**a.** They play 12 rounds of the game. How many points can Fred expect to win? How many points can Joseph expect to win?

**b.** How many points per round can each player expect to win? That is, what is the expected value for each player?

**c.** Is this a game in which Fred and Joseph have an equally-likely chance of making a winning total? Why or why not?

**21.** Ms. Rodriguez brought her dog to the vet for a distemper test. The test is correct 80% of the time. This means that 20% of the time the test of a dog with distemper indicates no distemper. The vet decides to test the dog twice.

**a.** If the dog has distemper, what is the probability that both tests will indicate no distemper? (It may help to make an area model of this situation.)

**b.** If the dog has distemper, what is the probability that at least one of the tests will indicate distemper?

**22.** A computer places a dot at random on a dartboard that is divided into four regions, A, B, C, and D. The dot has the same probability of being in region B, region C, or region D. The probability that the dot will be in region A is 40%.

**a.** What is the probability that the dot will *not* be in region A?

**b.** Make a square dartboard that meets the given conditions.

**c.** Make a circular dartboard that meets the given conditions.

# Extensions

**For Exercises 23 and 24, use the data about the basketball team from Exercises 3–5.**

**23.** What is the probability that Alex will make all of his next three free throws? Explain your reasoning.

**24.** David is in a one-and-one free-throw situation. What is the probability that he will make both free-throws?

**25.** Emilio increases his free-throw average to 50%. His coach makes a deal with him. At tomorrow's practice, Emilio can attempt either to make three free throws in a row or to make at least four out of five free throws. If he is successful, he will start every game for the rest of the season. Which option should he choose? Explain.

**26. a.** Curt has made 60% of his free throws during recent practice sessions. The coach says that if Curt makes three free throws in a row, he can start Saturday's game. What is the probability that Curt will start Saturday's game?

**b.** Curt has a difficult time making three free throws in a row. The coach tells him to instead try making three out of four free throws. What is the probability that Curt will make at least three out of four free throws?

**27.** Natalie designs a carnival spinner game with 38 congruent sectors; 18 orange, 18 blue, and 2 white. A player pays $1 to play. The player picks either orange or blue. If the spinner stops on the chosen color, the player wins $2. If the spinner lands on any other color, the player does not get any money.

**a.** What is the probability that a player will lose on one spin of the wheel?

**b.** If a player plays the game many times, what is the average amount of money the player can expect to win or lose per spin of the wheel?

**28.** When a player is fouled while attempting a three-point basket, three free throws are awarded. Luis has an 80% free-throw average. He draws the diagrams below to analyze the probability of getting 1, 2, or 3 baskets.

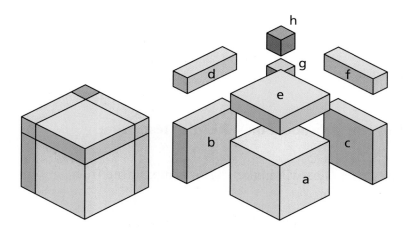

**a.** Which parts of the lettered diagram represent Luis making all three baskets? Exactly two baskets? Exactly one basket? Missing all three baskets?

**b.** What is the probability of Luis getting 1 point in a three free-throw situation? 2 points? 3 points? No points?

# Mathematical Reflections 3

**I**n this investigation, you learned how to find the average outcome for events, such as a basketball player attempting free throws in a one-and-one situation. The following questions will help you summarize what you have learned.

Think about your answers to these questions. Discuss your ideas with other students and your teacher. Then write a summary of your findings in your notebook.

**1.** Expected value is sometimes called the long-term average. Explain why this makes sense.

**2.** Describe how you would calculate the expected value for a probability situation.

**3.** Explain how expected value can be useful.

# Binomial Outcomes

## 4.1 Guessing Answers

**H**ave you ever forgotten to study for a quiz and had to guess at the answers? If you take a true/false quiz and guess on every question, what are your chances of getting every question right?

### Problem 4.1 Finding More Expected Values

A quiz has four true/false questions. Each question is worth 25 points.

- On a piece of paper, write the numbers 1 to 4 to represent the questions for the quiz.

- Toss a penny to determine the answer for each quiz item. Next to each number, write true (T) if a head shows and false (F) if a tail shows.

- After you have written your answers, your teacher will give you the correct answers.

- Mark your answers correct or incorrect. Record your score.

**A.** Compare answers with your classmates. How many papers had

   **1.** exactly 4 correct (all correct)

   **2.** exactly 3 correct (3 correct and 1 incorrect)

**3.** exactly 2 correct (2 correct and 2 incorrect)

**4.** exactly 1 correct (1 correct and 3 incorrect)

**5.** none correct (0 correct and 4 incorrect)

**B. 1.** If you guess on every question, how many different ways can you get exactly 1 incorrect answer? Exactly 2 incorrect answers? Exactly 3 incorrect answers? All 4 incorrect? All 4 correct?

   **2.** What is the probability of getting

   **a.** a score of 100 (all correct)

   **b.** a score of 75 (exactly three correct)

   **c.** a score of 50 (exactly two correct)

   **d.** a score of 25 (exactly one correct)

   **e.** a score of 0 (all incorrect)

**C. 1.** Suppose you take the quiz 32 times. How many times do you expect to get the given number of correct answers?

   **a.** 4     **b.** 3     **c.** 2     **d.** 1     **e.** 0

   **2.** What would your total score be in each case?

   **3.** If you take the quiz 32 times, what is the expected average score? Will the expected value change if you take the quiz 100 times? Explain.

**D.** Suppose the true/false quiz has five questions and you guess each one. What is the probability that you will get them all correct?

**ACE** **Homework starts on page 54.**

# Ortonville

**S**ituations like tossing a coin (or the true/false quiz) that have exactly two outcomes are binomial situations. The probability of getting one of two outcomes (like heads or tails) is called a **binomial probability.** In this problem, you will explore another binomial situation that has equally likely outcomes.

Ortonville is a very special town. Each family is named Orton and has exactly five children. The parents in Ortonville have agreed to call their children these names:

| The Orton Children | | |
| --- | --- | --- |
| | **Girl** | **Boy** |
| **First-Born Child** | Gloria | Benson |
| **Second-Born Child** | Gilda | Berndt |
| **Third-Born Child** | Gail | Blair |
| **Fourth-Born Child** | Gerry | Blake |
| **Fifth-Born Child** | Gina | Brett |

**A.** List all the possible outcomes for a family with five children.

**B.** What is the probability that a family has children named Gloria, Gilda, Blair, Blake, and Gina?

**C.** Find the probability that a family has

    **1.** exactly five girls or five boys

    **2.** two girls and three boys

    **3.** the first or last child a boy

    **4.** at least one boy

    **5.** at most one boy

**ACE** **Homework starts on page 54.**

# 4.3 A Baseball Series

Every fall the best baseball team in the American League plays the best team in the National League. The series has up to seven games. The first team to win four games wins the series.

# Problem 4.3 Expanding Binomial Probability

Suppose the Bobcats are playing the Gazelles in your town's little league "world series." The teams enter the series evenly matched. That is, they each have an equally likely chance of winning each game.

The Gazelles win the first two games of the series. The owner of the concession stands must predict how much food to order for the rest of the series. He needs to know the probability that the series will end in 4, 5, 6, or 7 games. To find the answer, he must find all the possible outcomes.

Label the outcomes with a G for a Gazelles win or a B for a Bobcats win. For example, BBGG means that the Bobcats win the third and fourth games and the Gazelles win the fifth and sixth games. In this example, the series ends in six games, when the Gazelles have won four games. Write G-6 after BBGG.

**A.** Before you analyze the rest of the series, predict whether it is more probable that the series will end in 4, 5, 6, or 7 games.

**B.** Suppose all five remaining games are played. What are all of the possible outcomes for these five games?

**C. 1.** For each outcome, determine the length of the series.

**2.** What is the probability that the series ends in four games? Five games? Six games? Seven games?

**D.** Analyze the outcomes in Question C for wins. What is the probability that the Gazelles win the series? That the Bobcats win the series?

**ACE** **Homework starts on page 54.**

## Did You Know?

The World Series started in 1903 as a best-of-nine-game series. From 1905 until 1919, the series changed to the best-of-seven games. After World War I ended, the series temporarily changed back to the best-of-nine games in 1919–1921. From 1922 until now, the series has remained a best-of-seven-game series. Between 1922 and 2003, the World Series ended in four games and five games both 15 times. It ended in six games 17 times and in seven games 34 times. There was no World Series in 1994.

**Go Online**
PHSchool.com  **For:** Information about the World Series
**Web Code:** ane-9031

## Applications

**1.** It costs six tickets to play the Toss-a-Penny game at the school carnival. For each turn, a player tosses a penny three times. If the penny lands heads up two or more times in a turn, the player wins ten tickets to spend on food and games.

   **a.** Suppose Benito plays the game 80 times. How many tickets can he expect to win?

   **b.** What is the average number of tickets Benito can expect to win or lose per turn?

**2. a.** If you toss three coins at the same time, is the probability of getting three heads the same as or different from the probability of getting three heads when you toss one coin three times in a row? Explain your reasoning.

   **b.** If you toss three coins and get three tails, what is the probability you will get three tails when you toss the three coins again? Explain.

**For Exercises 3–9, use this information: Scout, Ms. Rodriguez's dog, is about to have puppies. The vet thinks Scout will have four puppies. Assume that for each puppy, a male and female are equally likely.**

**3. a.** List all the possible combinations of female and male puppies Scout might have.

   **b.** Is Scout more likely to have four male puppies or two male and two female puppies? Explain.

**4. Multiple Choice** What is the probability that Scout will have four female puppies?

   **A.** $\frac{1}{2}$      **B.** $\frac{1}{4}$      **C.** $\frac{1}{8}$      **D.** $\frac{1}{16}$

**5. Multiple Choice** What is the probability that Scout will have two male and two female puppies?

   **F.** $\frac{1}{2}$      **G.** $\frac{1}{4}$      **H.** $\frac{1}{8}$      **J.** $\frac{6}{16}$

**6. Multiple Choice** What is the probability that Scout will have at least one male puppy?

   **A.** $\frac{15}{16}$      **B.** $\frac{7}{8}$      **C.** $\frac{3}{4}$      **D.** $\frac{1}{2}$

**7. Multiple Choice** What is the probability that Scout will have at least one female puppy?

F. $\frac{15}{16}$      G. $\frac{7}{8}$      H. $\frac{3}{4}$      J. $\frac{1}{2}$

**8.** Ms. Rodriguez plans to sell her dog's female puppies for $250 each and her male puppies for $200 each. How much money can she expect to make from a litter of four puppies?

**9.** Suppose the vet thinks Scout will have a litter of five puppies. How much money can Ms. Rodriguez expect to make from selling the puppies?

**10.** Rajan's class is holding a world series. They divide the class into two teams, which are evenly matched. One team is the Champs and the other team is the Stars. The series is five games, and the first team to win three games wins the series. The Champs win the first game.

   **a.** What is the probability that the series will end in 3, 4, or 5 games?

   **b.** What is the probability that the Stars will win the series?

# Connections

**11.** You might find that a tree diagram is a helpful model in this exercise.

   **a.** What are all the possible outcomes when you toss a coin three times?

   **b.** How many outcomes are there when you toss a coin four times? (You do not have to list them all.) Five times?

   **c.** How many ways can you get five heads in five tosses? How many ways can you get zero heads in five tosses? How many ways can you get four heads? One head? Three heads? Two heads?

   **d.** Explain why some symmetry in your answers in part (c) makes sense.

**Go Online**
PHSchool.com
**For:** Multiple-Choice Skills Practice
**Web Code:** ana-7454

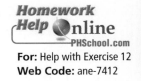
**12.** The largest hamster litter on record consisted of 26 babies. Suppose a hamster has 26 babies. Assume that the birth of a female and the birth of a male are equally likely. What is the theoretical probability that all 26 babies will be male? Explain your reasoning.

**13.** In the unit *How Likely Is It?*, you learned about genetics. Every person has a combination of two tongue-curling alleles, TT, Tt, or tt, where T is the dominant tongue-curling allele, and t is the recessive non-tongue-curling allele. A person with at least one T allele will be able to curl his or her tongue.

Kent found out that his tongue-curling alleles are tt and his wife Diane's alleles are Tt. He makes this table to help him determine the possible outcomes for their children.

**Kent**

|  | | t | t |
|---|---|---|---|
| **Diane** | T | Tt | Tt |
| | t | tt | tt |

The possible combinations are Tt, Tt, tt, and tt. This means that a child of Kent and Diane has a 50% chance of being able to curl his or her tongue.

**a.** Suppose Kent and Diane have two children. What is the probability that both of the children will be able to curl their tongues? Make a tree diagram to help you answer this question.

**b.** Suppose Kent and Diane have four children. What is the probability that none of the children will be able to curl their tongues?

**c.** Suppose Kent and Diane have four children. What is the probability that only the oldest child will be able to curl his or her tongue?

**14.** King George's home, Castle Warwick, is under siege. King George must escape to his cousin's home, Castle Howard. The only escape route is through a series of canals, shown below.

There are five gates in the series of canals. Each gate opens and closes at random and is open half the time and closed the other half. The arrows show the way the water is flowing.

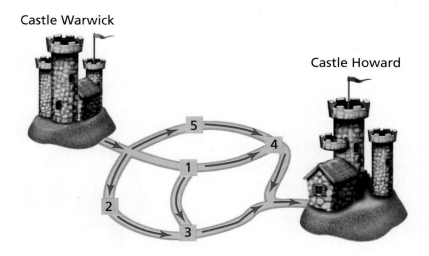

**Castle Warwick**

**Castle Howard**

  **a.** What is the probability that a water route from Castle Warwick to Castle Howard is open?

  **b.** How is this exercise similar to Problem 4.3?

**15.** Drew, the paper carrier, collects $10 per week from each customer for the paper. One customer offers him these deals.

  **a.** Toss five coins. If there are four or more heads, the customer pays $18. Otherwise, he pays $4. Find the expected value for this deal. Decide if it is a fair deal.

  **b.** Toss five coins. If they are all the same, the customer pays $80. Otherwise, he pays $4. Find the expected value for this deal. Decide if it is a fair deal.

**16.** Ethan makes a game played on the number line. At the start of a turn, a player places a marker on 0. The player tosses a penny and moves the marker one unit to the right if the penny lands heads up and one unit to the left if it lands tails up. A turn is three tosses, and the score for that turn is the number naming the location of the marker at the end of that turn.

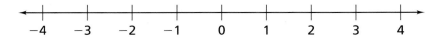

**a.** What scores are possible after one turn (three tosses)?

**b.** Suppose Ethan changes his game so that a turn consists of four tosses. What scores would be possible after one turn?

**17. a.** Spinning the pointer at the right once makes a binomial situation. What are the possible outcomes of a single spin? What is the probability of each outcome?

**b.** Spinning the spinner from part (a) three times is also a binomial situation. If the result of the first spin is Red, does this affect the possible outcomes of the second and third spins? What is the probability of RBB (in this order), assuming each spin is independent of the previous spin?

**c.** Using the spinner at the right once is *not* a binomial situation. What are the possible outcomes? What is the probability of each?

**d.** Does spinning the spinner at the right make a binomial situation? Explain.

**e.** Suppose you spin the spinner in part (d) three times. What is the probability of RBB (in this order)?

# Extensions

Pascal's Triangle (on the left, below) can be used to summarize binomial probabilities and answer new questions in some binomial situations. The sum of each row is the same as the number of outcomes in a binomial probability. For example, some binomial situations are written across from their corresponding row.

| Pascal's Triangle | | | | | | | Coin | True/False Test |
|---|---|---|---|---|---|---|---|---|
| | | | 1 | | | | | |
| | | 1 | | 1 | | | Tossing 1 coin | 1 question |
| | 1 | | 2 | | 1 | | Tossing 2 coins | 2 questions |
| 1 | | 3 | | 3 | | 1 | Tossing 3 coins | 3 questions |
| 1 | 4 | | 6 | | 4 | 1 | Tossing 4 coins | 4 questions |
| 1 | 5 | 10 | | 10 | 5 | 1 | Tossing 5 coins | 5 questions |

**18.** Describe some patterns in Pascal's Triangle.

**19.** What is the sixth row (the next row in the diagram above) of Pascal's Triangle? Describe what probabilities each number represents in a situation that involves tossing 6 coins.

**In your answers for Exercises 20–22, tell which row from Pascal's Triangle you used.**

**20.** On a five-question true/false test, what is the probability that you will guess exactly two correct answers?

**21.** A coin is tossed six times. What is the probability that at least two heads occur?

**22.** On a nine-question true/false test, what is the probability that you will guess exactly three correct answers?

# Mathematical Reflections 4

**I**n this investigation, you looked at probabilities for situations involving a series of actions, each with two equally likely outcomes. The following questions will help you summarize what you have learned.

Think about your answers to these questions. Discuss your ideas with other students and your teacher. Then write a summary of your findings in your notebook.

1. Describe five different binomial situations. Explain why they are binomial situations.

2. Tossing a coin three times is an example of a situation involving a series of three actions, each with two equally likely outcomes.

   **a.** Pick one of the situations you described in Question 1. Describe a series of three actions, each with two equally likely outcomes. Make a list of all the possible outcomes.

   **b.** Write a question about your situation that can be answered by your list.

3. As you increase the number of actions for a binomial situation, what happens to the total number of possible outcomes? For example, if you increase the number of times a coin is tossed, what happens to the total number of outcomes?

# Unit Project

## The Carnival Game

**T**his project requires you to use the mathematics you have studied in several units, including this one. You will make a game for a school carnival and test your game. Then, you will write a report about your game.

### Part 1: Design a Carnival Game

You can design a new game or redesign one of the games you analyzed in this unit. Keep these guidelines in mind.

- The game should make a profit for the school.
- The game should be easy to set up and use at a school carnival. It should not require expensive equipment.
- The game should take a relatively short time to play.
- The rules should be easily understood by people your age.

### Part 2: Test Your Game

After you have drafted a game design, play the game several times until you feel confident that you can predict what will happen in the long run. Keep track of your trials, and include that information in your report.

### Part 3: Submit Your Design to the Carnival Committee

Once you are satisfied that your game is reasonable, prepare to submit your design. Your submission to the committee should include two things: a model or a scale model of the game and a written report.

### Model or Scale Model

If you build a scale model instead of an actual model, give the scale factor from the scale model to the actual game.

You can either construct the model out of similar materials to those you would use for the actual game, or you can prepare scale drawings of the game. If you make drawings, be sure to include enough views of your game so that anyone could look at the drawings and construct the game.

### Report

Include a set of rules that explains how the game is played, how much it costs to play, how a player wins, and how much a player wins.

## Part 4: Write a Report

Write a report about your game to the carnival committee. Assume that the committee consists of teachers in the building (not just mathematics teachers), parents, and other students. Your report should include:

- The experimental probability of winning the game that you found from playing the game several times. If possible, give the theoretical probability as well. If you don't give the theoretical probability of winning your game, explain why you did not.

- The amount of money the school will collect and how much they should expect to pay out if the game is played many times. Explain how you determined these amounts.

- An explanation of why your game should be chosen. Explain why the game is worth having in the carnival and why you think people would want to play it.

# Looking Back and Looking Ahead

In this unit, you studied some basic ideas of probability and some ways to use those ideas to solve problems about probability and expected value. In particular, you studied how to

**Go Online**
PHSchool.com

**For:** Vocabulary Review Puzzle
**Web Code:** anj-7051

- find and interpret experimental and theoretical probabilities
- use simulations to gather experimental data
- use tree diagrams, and other listing techniques to find all of the possible outcomes
- use area models in which probabilities are shown as parts of a whole square or circle

## Use Your Understanding: Probability Reasoning

To test your understanding and skill with probability ideas and strategies, consider the following problem situations.

**1.** Maria's homework problem is to design two dartboards that match these conditions:

- The probability of landing in region A is 30%.
- The probability of landing in region B is 25%.
- The probability of landing in region C is 20%.
- The remaining space on the dartboard is region D.

  **a.** Draw a square dartboard that meets the given conditions.

  **b.** Draw a circular dartboard that meets the given conditions.

  **c.** For each dartboard, find the probability that a dart will

   **i.** land in region D

   **ii.** land in a region other than D

   **iii.** *not* land in region A

**2.** Gabrielle and Jim are playing the Match/No Match game. On each turn, the players spin the two spinners shown below. Gabrielle scores 1 point if the spins match, and Jim scores 1 point if they do not match.

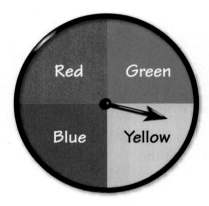 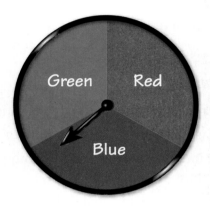

**a.** Use a tree diagram to show all the possible outcomes for this game.

**b.** What is the theoretical probability of getting a match?

**c.** What is the theoretical probability of getting a non-match?

**d.** Does each player have an equally-likely chance of winning?

**e.** Is this a fair game? If so, explain why. If not, explain how you could change the rules to make it fair.

**3.** Kali and Antonio designed a new computer game. They programmed the game so the probability that a player will win is $\frac{1}{4}$ on each turn. If the player wins, the score increases by four points. If the player loses, two points are deducted from the score.

**a.** Matthew plans to play 12 rounds of the game. How many points can he expect to score?

**b.** How many points per round can Matthew expect to win or lose?

**c.** Is this a fair game? If not, how would you change the points won or lost so that it is a fair game?

## Explain Your Reasoning

When you use mathematical calculations or diagrams to solve a problem or make a decision, it is important to justify your reasoning. Answer these questions about your work.

**4.** What does it mean to say that the probability of an event is $\frac{1}{2}$ or $\frac{2}{3}$ or $\frac{5}{8}$?

**5.** How are experimental and theoretical probabilities of an event related to each other?

**6.** Explain and illustrate with specific examples how you could use each strategy to analyze probabilities.

   **a.** tree diagrams            **b.** area models

**7.** What does it mean to find the expected value of a chance activity with numerical outcomes? Give three examples of problems in this unit for which you had to find the expected value.

## Look Ahead

You will almost certainly meet the ideas about probability of this unit in future study and problem solving in mathematics, science, and questions about games of chance. These are the basis of statistical reasoning that will be developed in the *Connected Mathematics* unit, *Samples and Populations,* and which you will see in areas as diverse as genetics, the payoffs in state lotteries, and local fundraisers.

## A

**area model** A diagram in which fractions of the area of the diagram correspond to probabilities in a situation. For example, suppose there are three blue blocks and two red blocks in a container. If two blocks are drawn out, one at a time, replacing the block drawn each time, the area model below shows that the probability of getting two red blocks is $\frac{4}{25}$.

Area models are particularly helpful when the outcomes being analyzed are not equally likely, because more likely outcomes take up larger areas. Area models are also helpful for outcomes involving more than one stage, such as rolling a number cube, then tossing a coin or choosing a bag, then drawing a block from it.

**modelo por áreas** Un diagrama en el que las fracciones del área del diagrama corresponden a las probabilidades en una situación. Por ejemplo, si hay tres bloques azules y dos bloques rojos en un recipiente y se saca un bloque cada vez sin reemplazarlo, el modelo por áreas de abajo muestra que la probabilidad de sacar dos bloques rojos es $\frac{4}{25}$.

Los modelos por áreas son especialmente útiles cuando los resultados que se analizan no son igualmente probables, porque los resultados más probables tienen áreas más grandes. Los modelos por áreas son también útiles para resultados que incluyen más de un paso, como tirar un cubo numérico y luego tirar una moneda, o elegir una bolsa y luego sacar un bloque de ella.

**Second Choice**

|  |  | B | B | B | R | R |
|---|---|---|---|---|---|---|
| **First Choice** | B | BB | BB | BB | BR | BR |
|  | B | BB | BB | BB | BR | BR |
|  | B | BB | BB | BB | BR | BR |
|  | R | RB | RB | RB | RR | RR |
|  | R | RB | RB | RB | RR | RR |

## B

**binomial probability** The probability of getting one of two outcomes (like heads or tails).

**probabilidad binomial** La probabilidad de obtener uno de dos resultados (como cara o cruz).

## E

**equally likely** Two or more events that have the same probability of occurring. For example, when you toss a fair coin, heads and tails are equally likely; each has a 50% chance of happening. Rolling a six-sided number cube gives a $\frac{1}{6}$ probability for each number to come up. Each outcome is equally likely.

**igualmente probables** Dos o más sucesos que tienen la misma probabilidad de ocurrir. Por ejemplo, cuando se lanza una moneda "justa" la probabilidad de obtener cara es igual a la de obtener cruz; es decir, cada caso tiene una probabilidad del 50%. Tirar un cubo numérico de 6 lados supone $\frac{1}{6}$ de probabilidad de que salga cada número. Cada resultado es igualmente probable

**expected value (or long-term average)**
Intuitively, the average payoff over the long run. For example, suppose you are playing a game with two number cubes. You score 2 points when a sum of 6 is rolled, 1 point for a sum of 3, and 0 points for anything else. If you roll the cubes 36 times, you could expect to roll a sum of 6 about five times and a sum of 3 about twice. This means that you could expect to score $(5 \times 2) + (2 \times 1) = 12$ points for 36 rolls, an average of $\frac{12}{36} = \frac{1}{3}$ point per roll. Here, $\frac{1}{3}$ is the expected value (or average over the long run) of one roll.

**valor esperado (o promedio a largo plazo)** El promedio de puntos o la recompensa conseguidos tras realizar muchos intentos. Por ejemplo, imagínate un juego con dos cubos numéricos en el que obtienes 2 puntos por una suma de 6, 1 punto por una suma de 3 y 0 puntos por cualquier otra suma. Si lanzaras los cubos numéricos 36 veces, sería de esperar que obtuvieras una suma de 6 aproximadamente cinco veces y una de 3 aproximadamente dos veces. Es decir, cabría esperar conseguir $(5 \times 2) + (2 \times 1) = 12$ puntos en los 36 lanzamientos, o sea un promedio de $\frac{12}{36} = \frac{1}{3}$ punto por lanzamiento. Aquí $\frac{1}{3}$ es el valor esperado (o promedio a largo plazo) de un lanzamiento.

**experimental probability** A probability that is determined through experimentation. For example, you could find the experimental probability of getting a head when you toss a coin by tossing a coin many times and keeping track of the outcomes. The experimental probability would be the ratio of the number of heads to the total number of tosses, or trials. Experimental probability may not be the same as the theoretical probability. However, for a large number of trials, they are likely to be close. Experimental probabilities can be used to predict behavior over the long run.

**probabilidad experimental** La probabilidad determinada mediante la experimentación. Por ejemplo, para hallar la probabilidad experimental de obtener cara en el lanzamiento de una moneda, podrías efectuar numerosos lanzamientos y anotar los resultados. Dicha probabilidad sería la razón entre el número de caras y el número de lanzamientos, o intentos. La probabilidad experimental puede no ser igual a la probabilidad teórica. Sin embargo, es probable que estén muy cerca durante muchos lanzamientos. Las probabilidades experimentales sirven para predecir lo que ocurrirá a largo plazo.

**F**

**fair game** A game in which each player is equally likely to win. The probability of winning a two-person fair game is $\frac{1}{2}$. An unfair game can be made fair by adjusting the scoring system, or the payoffs. For example, suppose you play a game in which two fair coins are tossed. You score when both coins land heads up. Otherwise, your opponent scores. The probability that you will score is $\frac{1}{4}$, and the probability that your opponent will score is $\frac{3}{4}$. To make the game fair, you might adjust the scoring system so that you receive 3 points each time you score and your opponent receives 1 point when he or she scores. This would make the expected values for each player equal, which results in a fair game.

**juego justo** Un juego en el que cada jugador tiene igual probabilidad de ganar. La probabilidad de ganar en un juego justo entre dos personas es $\frac{1}{2}$. Para hacer justo un juego que no lo es, se puede ajustar el sistema de reparto de puntos o de recompensas. Por ejemplo, imagina un juego que consiste en lanzar dos monedas "justas". Si salen dos caras, tú obtienes puntos. Si no, los obtiene el otro jugador. La probabilidad de que tú consigas los puntos es $\frac{1}{4}$ y la probabilidad de que los consiga el otro jugador es $\frac{3}{4}$. Para hacer justo el juego, podrías ajustar el sistema de reparto de puntos de manera que, cada vez que salgan dos caras, tú recibas 3 puntos y en las demás ocasiones el otro jugador reciba 1 punto. Esto haría que los valores esperados para cada jugador fueran iguales, lo que resulta en un juego justo.

## L

**Law of Large Numbers** This law states, in effect, that as more trials of an experiment are conducted, the experimental probability more closely approximates the theoretical probability. It is not at all unusual to have 100% heads after three tosses of a fair coin, but it would be extremely unusual to have even 60% heads after 1,000 tosses. This is expressed by the Law of Large Numbers.

**Ley de números grandes** Esta ley enuncia, en efecto, que cuantos más intentos de un experimento se realizan, más se aproximará la probabilidad experimental a la teórica. No es inusual tener 100% caras después de tres lanzamientos de una moneda justa, pero sería extremadamente inusual tener incluso 60% de caras después de 1,000 lanzamientos. Esto se expresa con la Ley de números grandes.

## O

**outcome** A possible result. For example, when a number cube is rolled, the possible outcomes are 1, 2, 3, 4, 5, and 6. Other possible outcomes are even or odd. Others are three and not three. When determining probabilities, it is important to be clear about what the possible outcomes are.

**resultado** Consecuencia posible. Por ejemplo, cuando se lanza un cubo numérico, los resultados posibles son 1, 2, 3, 4, 5 y 6. Otros resultados posibles son pares o impares. Otros son es tres y no tres. Cuando se determinan las probabilidades, es importante definir cuáles son los resultados posibles.

## P

**payoff** The number of points (or dollars or other objects of value) a player in a game receives for a particular outcome.

**recompensa** El número de puntos (o dólares u otros objetos de valor) que recibe un jugador por un resultado particular.

**probability** A number between 0 and 1 that describes the likelihood that an outcome will occur. For example, when a fair number cube is rolled, a 2 can be expected $\frac{1}{6}$ of the time, so the probability of rolling a 2 is $\frac{1}{6}$. The probability of a certain outcome is 1, while the probability of an impossible outcome is 0.

**probabilidad** Un número comprendido entre 0 y 1 que indica la probabilidad de que ocurra un suceso. Por ejemplo, cuando se lanza un cubo numérico justo, se puede esperar un 2 cada $\frac{1}{6}$ de las veces, por lo que la probabilidad de que salga un 2 es $\frac{1}{6}$. La probabilidad de un suceso seguro es 1, mientras que la probabilidad de un suceso imposible es 0.

## R

**random** Outcomes that are uncertain when viewed individually, but which exhibit a predictable pattern over many trials, are random. For example, when you roll a fair number cube, you have no way of knowing what the next roll will be, but you do know that, over the long run, you will roll each number on the cube about the same number of times.

**sucesos aleatorios** Aquellos sucesos cuyos resultados, al considerarse separadamente, no son seguros, pero que podrían presentar un patrón previsible al observarse a lo largo de muchos intentos. Por ejemplo, en el caso de lanzar un cubo numérico perfecto es imposible saber cuál será el resultado del próximo lanzamiento; sin embargo, sí se sabe que a la larga saldrá cada uno de los números del cubo numérico aproximadamente la misma cantidad de veces.

## S

**sample space** The set of all possible outcomes in a probability situation. When you toss two coins, the sample space consists of four outcomes: HH, HT, TH, and TT.

**espacio muestral** El conjunto de todos los resultados posibles en una probabilidad. Cuando lanzas dos monedas, el espacio muestral son cuatro resultados: CC, CX, XC y XX.

**theoretical probability** A probability obtained by analyzing a situation. If all of the outcomes are equally likely, you can find a theoretical probability of an event by listing all of the possible outcomes and then finding the ratio of the number of outcomes producing the desired event to the total number of outcomes. For example, there are 36 possible equally likely outcomes (number pairs) when two fair number cubes are rolled. Of these, six have a sum of 7, so the probability of rolling a sum of 7 is $\frac{6}{36}$, or $\frac{1}{6}$.

**probabilidad teórica** La probabilidad obtenida mediante el análisis de una situación. Si todos los resultados de un suceso son igualmente probables, entonces para hallar la probabilidad teórica del mismo se escribe una lista de todos los resultados posibles y luego se halla la razón entre el número de resultados que produce el suceso deseado para el número total de resultados. Por ejemplo, al lanzar dos cubos numéricos perfectos existen 36 resultados igualmente probables (pares de números). De ellos, seis tienen una suma de 7, por lo que la probabilidad de obtener una suma de 7 es $\frac{6}{36}$, o sea, $\frac{1}{6}$.

**tree diagram** A diagram used to determine the number of possible outcomes in a probability situation. The number of final branches is equal to the number of possible outcomes. The tree diagram below shows all the possible outcomes for randomly choosing a yellow or red rose and then a white or pink ribbon. The four possible outcomes are listed in the last column. Tree diagrams are handy to use when outcomes are equally likely.

**diagrama de árbol** Un diagrama que se utiliza para determinar el número de resultados posibles en una situación de probabilidad. El número de ramas finales es igual al número de resultados posibles. El siguiente diagrama de árbol muestra todos los resultados posibles al escoger al azar una rosa amarilla o roja, y luego una cinta blanca o rosada. Los cuatro resultados posibles aparecen en la última columna. Los diagramas de árbol son útiles cuando los resultados son igualmente probables..

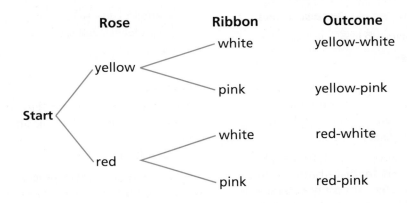

# Academic Vocabulary

The following terms are important to your understanding of the mathematics in this unit. Knowing and using these words will help you in thinking, reasoning, representing, communicating your ideas, and making connections across ideas. When these words make sense to you, the investigations and problems will make more sense as well.

**D**

**describe** To explain or tell in detail. A written description can contain facts and other information needed to communicate your answer. A diagram or a graph may also be included.
*related terms: express, explain*

**Sample: Three of ten rolls of a number cube result in a 5. Describe the theoretical and experimental probability of rolling a 5.**

> Since a number cube has six equal sides and the number 5 appears once, the theoretical probability of rolling a 5 is $\frac{1}{6}$. The experimental probability of rolling a 5 is $\frac{3}{10}$.

**describir** Explicar o decir con detalle. Una descripción escrita puede contener hechos y otra información necesaria para comunicar tu respuesta. También se puede incluir un diagrama o una gráfica.
*términos relacionados: expresar, explicar*

**Ejemplo: Tres de 10 tiros de un dado numérico resultan en un 5. Describe la probabilidad teórica y experimental de que salga un 5.**

> Como un cubo numérico tiene seis caras iguales y el número 5 aparece una sola vez, la probabilidad teórica de que salga un 5 es $\frac{1}{6}$. La probabilidad experimental de que salga un 5 es $\frac{3}{10}$.

**determine** To use the given information and any related facts to find a value or make a decision.
*related terms: solve, evaluate, examine*

**Sample: Eugene's favorite shirts are red, black, orange, and white. His favorite hats are red, gold, and black. Eugene randomly selects one shirt and one hat. Make a chart to determine the probability that they are the same color.**

> The chart shows 12 possible combinations. The probability of the same color is $\frac{2}{12}$, or $\frac{1}{6}$.
>
> |  |  | **Hats** | |
> |---|---|---|---|
> |  | R | G | B |
> | R | RR | RG | RB |
> | B | BR | BG | BB |
> | O | OR | OG | OB |
> | W | WR | WG | WB |
>
> (Shirts)

**determinar** Usar la información dada y cualesquiera datos relacionados para hallar un valor o tomar una decisión.
*términos relacionados: resolver, evaluar, examinar*

**Ejemplo: Las camisetas favoritas de Eugene son rojas, negras, anaranjadas y blancas. Sus sombreros favoritos son rojos, dorados y negros. Eugene selecciona al azar una camiseta y un sombrero. Haz una tabla para determinar la probabilidad de que sean del mismo color.**

> La tabla muestra 12 combinaciones posibles. La probabilidad de que sean del mismo color es de $\frac{2}{12}$ ó $\frac{1}{6}$.
>
> |  |  | **Sombreros** | |
> |---|---|---|---|
> |  | R | D | N |
> | R | RR | RD | RN |
> | N | NR | ND | NN |
> | A | AR | AD | AN |
> | B | BR | BD | BN |
>
> (Camisetas)

**design** To make using specific criteria.
*related terms: draw, plan, outline, model*

**Sample: Nils invented a computer game which randomly hides a treasure chest. The probability that the treasure chest will be hidden in the sand is 50%, in the water 30%, in the rocks 10%, or in the grass 10%. Design a computer screen that Nils could use for his game.**

I'll draw 50 of the 100 square units as sand, 30 as water, and 10 each as rocks and grass to match each probability.

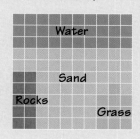

Water
Sand
Rocks
Grass

**diseñar** Hacer siguiendo un criterio específico.
*términos relacionados: dibujar, planear, bosquejar, modelar*

**Ejemplo: Nils inventó un juego de computadora que aleatoriamente esconde un cofre lleno de tesoro. La probabilidad de que el cofre esté escondido en la arena es del 50%, en el agua del 30%, en las rocas 10% o en el pasto del 10%. Diseña una pantalla de computadora que Nils pudiera usar para su juego.**

Dibujaré 50 de los 100 cuadrados unitarios para la arena, 30 para el agua, 10 para las rocas y 10 para el pasto, para representar cada probabilidad.

Agua
Arena
Rocas
Pasto

---

**explain** To give facts and details that make an idea easier to understand. Explaining can involve a written summary supported by a diagram, chart, table, or a combination of these.
*related terms: describe, clarify, describe, justify*

**Sample: Find the probability of tossing a coin 3 times and getting heads exactly two times. Explain your reasoning.**

I can use a tree diagram to look at all eight possible outcomes when tossing a coin three times.

| Toss 1 | Toss 2 | Toss 3 | Results |
|--------|--------|--------|---------|
| H | H | H | HHH |
|   |   | T | **HHT** |
|   | T | H | **HTH** |
|   |   | T | HTT |
| T | H | H | **THH** |
|   |   | T | THT |
|   | T | H | TTH |
|   |   | T | TTT |

There are 3 outcomes in which there are exactly two heads. The probability is $\frac{3}{8}$.

**explicar** Dar datos y detalles que facilitan el entendimiento de una idea. Explicar puede requerir la preparación de un informe escrito apoyado por información basada en un diagrama, una tabla, un esquema o una combinación de éstos.
*términos relacionados: describir, aclarar, justificar*

**Ejemplo: Halla la probabilidad de tirar una moneda al aire 3 veces y que caiga cara exactamente dos veces. Explica tu razonamiento.**

Puedo usar un diagrama arborescente para observar los ocho resultados posibles al tirar una moneda al aire tres veces.

| Tirada 1 | Tirada 2 | Tirada 3 | Resultados |
|----------|----------|----------|------------|
| Ca | Ca | Ca | CaCaCa |
|    |    | Cr | **CaCaCr** |
|    | Cr | Ca | **CaCrCa** |
|    |    | Cr | CaCrCr |
| Cr | Ca | Ca | **CrCaCa** |
|    |    | Cr | CrCaCr |
|    | Cr | Ca | CrCrCa |
|    |    | Cr | CrCrCr |

Hay 3 resultados en que hay exactamente dos caras. La probabilidad es de $\frac{3}{8}$.

# Index

Index

# Acknowledgments

## Team Credits

The people who made up the **Connected Mathematics 2** team—representing editorial, editorial services, design services, and production services—are listed below. Bold type denotes core team members.

Leora Adler, Judith Buice, Kerry Cashman, Patrick Culleton, Sheila DeFazio, Katie Hallahan, Richard Heater, **Barbara Hollingdale, Jayne Holman,** Karen Holtzman, **Etta Jacobs,** Christine Lee, Carolyn Lock, Catherine Maglio, **Dotti Marshall,** Rich McMahon, Eve Melnechuk, Kristin Mingrone, Terri Mitchell, **Marsha Novak,** Irene Rubin, Donna Russo, Robin Samper, Siri Schwartzman, **Nancy Smith,** Emily Soltanoff, **Mark Tricca,** Paula Vergith, Roberta Warshaw, Helen Young

## Additional Credits

Diana Bonfilio, Mairead Reddin, Michael Torocsik, nSight, Inc.

## Technical Illustration

WestWords, Inc.

## Cover Design

tom white.images

## Photographs

Every effort has been made to secure permission and provide appropriate credit for photographic material. The publisher deeply regrets any omission and pledges to correct errors called to its attention in subsequent editions.

Unless otherwise acknowledged, all photographs are the property of Pearson Education, Inc.

Photo locators denoted as follows: Top (T), Center (C), Bottom (B), Left (L), Right (R), Background (Bkgd)

**2** PCN Chrome/Alamy (B) Comstock/Getty Images; **3** Bill Frymire/Masterfile Corporation; **5** Lisette Le Bon/SuperStock; **14** Jack Hollingsworth/Corbis; **28** Peter Beck/Corbis; **32** Stockbyte/Getty Images; **40** PCN Chrome/Alamy; **44** Philip James Corwin/Corbis; **47** Larry Williams/Corbis; **50** Comstock/Getty Images; **53** Jed Jacobsohn/Getty Images; **55** Ron Kimball/Kimball Stock; **56** Hans Reinhard/Corbis

## Data Sources

Grateful acknowledgement is made to the following for copyrighted material:

### Sports Illustrated

"*Sports People: Don Calhoun*" by Lisa Bessone from SPORTS ILLUSTRATED, APRIL 26, 1993, 48. Used by permission. (p 38)

### Guinness World Records, Ltd.

"*Largest Hamster Litter on Record*" from GUINNESS BOOK OF WORLD RECORDS 2003. Courtesy of Guinness World Records, Ltd. (p 56)